US NAVAL AVIATION

IN THE 1980s

MARINE CORPS, NAVAL TRAINING, TEST AND RESERVE AIR STATIONS

Adrian Symonds

AMBERLEY

Acknowledgements

I would like to thank Sally Tunnicliffe for her assistance. Special thanks go to my wife, Louise, and son, Charlie.

This book is dedicated to the men and women of US Naval Aviation.

First published 2023

Amberley Publishing
The Hill, Stroud
Gloucestershire, GL5 4EP

www.amberley-books.com

Copyright © Adrian Symonds, 2023

The right of Adrian Symonds to be identified as the Author of this work has been asserted in accordance with the Copyrights, Designs and Patents Act 1988.

ISBN 978 1 3981 1101 1 (print)
ISBN 978 1 3981 1102 8 (ebook)

British Library Cataloguing in Publication Data. A catalogue record for this book is available from the British Library.

Typesetting by SJmagic DESIGN SERVICES, India. Printed in the UK.

Contents

Introduction

This is the second of two volumes covering United States Naval Aviation during the 1980s. While the first volume covered United States Navy (USN) Atlantic Fleet and Pacific Fleet Air Stations, this volume will cover Naval Education and Training Command, Naval Air Reserve, Naval Air Systems Command and United States Marine Corps (USMC) air stations.

In the following descriptions, unit identification letter 'tailcodes' are noted in parenthesis after squadron or wing, as appropriate.

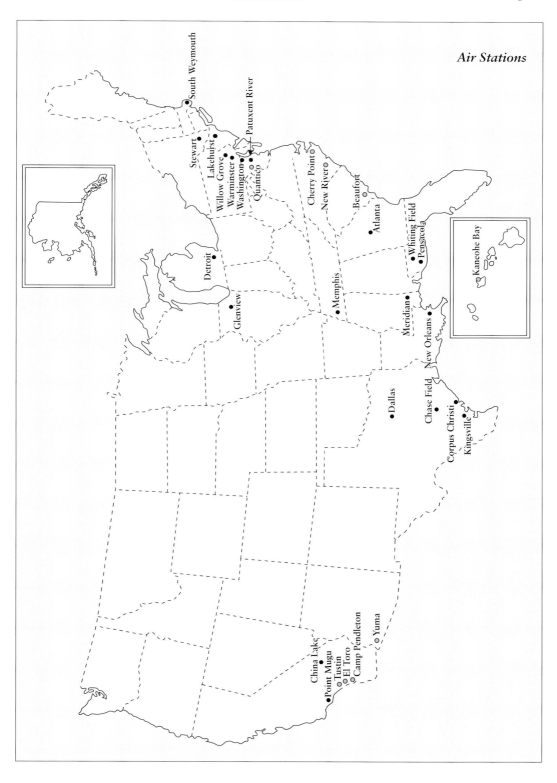

Air Stations

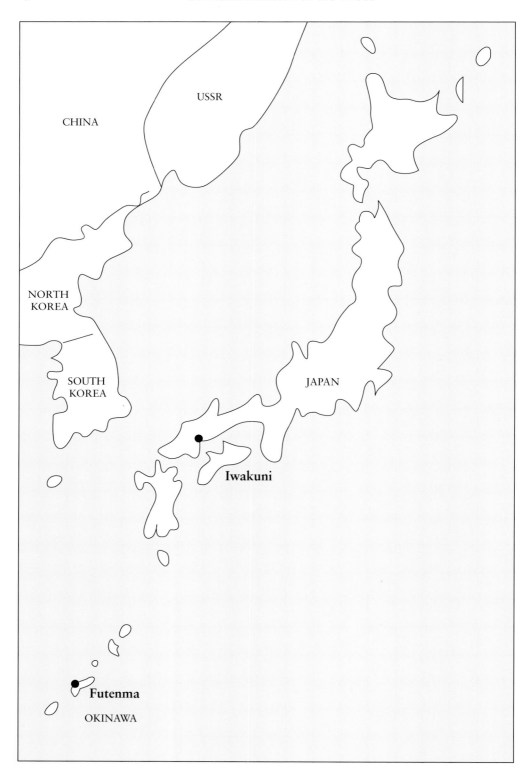

USSR

CHINA

NORTH
KOREA

SOUTH
KOREA

JAPAN

Iwakuni

Futenma

OKINAWA

Naval Education and Training Command Stations

The Chief of Naval Air Training (CNATRA), located at Corpus Christi, reported to Chief of Naval Education and Training (CNET), located at Pensacola. CNET commanded Naval Education and Training Command (NETC). CNATRA trained 2,000 pilots ('naval aviators') and Naval Flight Officers (NFOs) per year. NFOs were non-pilot flight crew members, including F-4/F-14 Radar Intercept Officers (RIOs), A-6 Bombardier/Navigators (B/Ns) and EA-6B Electronic Countermeasures Officers (ECMOs), etc. There were three routes of entry for these students. Those who completed a four-year university-equivalent course at the US Naval Academy at Annapolis, Maryland, and those who completed a Naval Reserve Officer Training Candidate Scholarship at a mainstream university or college, entered the USN as ensigns. Meanwhile, those who entered via the Aviation Officer Candidate Program, which put enlisted men or civilians through the Officer Candidate School at Pensacola, became reserve ensigns.

After completing the six-week Aviation Preflight Indoctrination (API) course, students were streamed for pilot or NFO training.

Pilot training started with twenty weeks of Primary Flight Training on T-34Cs, following which they were further streamed. Pilots destined for jets undertook a twenty-four-week Basic Jet course on T-2Cs, followed by a twenty-one-week Advanced Jet course on TA-4Js, the latter including carrier qualifications (CARQUALS). After land-based Field Carrier Landing Practice (FCLP), CARQUALS consisted of two touch-and-go landings, four arrested landings and four catapult launches at sea. Following successful completion of these courses, and having received their 'Wings of Gold', they were posted to the Fleet Replacement Squadron (FRS) for the type to which they are assigned, including the F-4, F-14, F/A-18, A-6, A-7, EA-6B, S-3, C-9 and OV-10. Those pilots streamed towards the C-2, E-2, P-3 and C-130 progressed from Primary Flight Training to a five-week Intermediate Prop course on T-34Cs, followed by the nineteen-week Multi-Engine course on T-44s. Pilots streamed towards helicopters conducted the same T-34C Intermediate Prop course, before progressing to the six-week Helicopter Transition course on TH-57s followed by the twelve-week Advanced Helicopter course on TH-1s/UH-1s or TH-57s.

NFO training began with a fifteen-week Basic course on T-34Cs and T-2Cs. Those then streamed towards the C-130 or P-3 were next sent to the Interservice Undergraduate Navigator Training (IUNT) course with the United States Air Force (USAF) on T-43s. All remaining NFOs undertook the seven-week Intermediate Course on the T-2B/C and T-29D/T-47A at Pensacola. Following this, NFOs destined to be airborne tactical data systems officers aboard E-2s were sent to an E-2 FRS. However, other NFOs remained at Pensacola for further training. For example, those destined to be F-4/F-14 RIOs spent another seventeen weeks on T-2B/Cs and T-29D/T-47As; prospective A-6 B/Ns remained at Pensacola for a further eleven weeks; prospective EA-6B ECMOs conducted the same eleven-week course as A-6 B/Ns, then followed up with a twelve-week Electronic Warfare Course.

Also under CNET was the Chief of Naval Technical Training (CNTECHTRA). CNTECHTRA's responsibilities included training air traffic controllers, aviation engineers and technical officers and enlisted personnel.

The increasing numbers of female pilots and NFOs were limited to duty with shore-based squadrons once they completed training; only those serving with carrier on-board delivery (COD) squadrons would get to trap aboard operational carriers.

Naval Air Station (NAS) Chase Field, Texas

Aboard Chase Field was Training Wing Three (TRAWING THREE/TW-3; identification letter C), which conducted intermediate (T-2C) and advanced (TA-4J) strike jet naval aviator training. Like other Training Wings, TRAWING THREE reported to CNATRA. TRAWING THREE controlled three Training Squadrons: VT-24 and VT-25 operated TA-4Js, while VT-26 operated T-2Cs. TRAWING THREE was assigned fifty-nine TA-4Js in 1980, numbers fluctuating around sixty for most of the decade, but increasing to sixty-six in 1988. Fifty-one T-2Cs were assigned in 1980, increasing to fifty-five during 1981 and peaking at sixty in 1983. By 1989 TRAWING THREE operated sixty-five TA-4Js and fifty-four T-2Cs.

Chase Field furnished limited support to Naval Auxiliary Landing Field (NALF) Goliad, located 16 miles north of Chase Field, and McMullen Target Range 66 miles west of Chase Field.

T-2C Buckeyes aboard USS *Lexington* (AVT-16) during pilot carrier training on 1 April 1989 in the Gulf of Mexico. Two T-2Cs sit behind the jet blast deflector (JBD) awaiting their turn on the catapult. The nearest aircraft is from TRAWING THREE's VT-26 'Tigers'; behind is a TRAWING ONE T-2C. A further T-2C is just visible on the catapult, while on the far corner of the flight deck a C-2A Greyhound and a US Coast Guard HH-65A Dolphin are visible. (National Archives and Records Administration)

A TRAWING THREE TA-4J Skyhawk awaits its turn on the catapult behind the JBD aboard *Lexington* on 1 April 1989; in the background a TRAWING ONE/VT-7 TA-4J climbs out after launching from *Lexington's* waist catapult. (NARA)

Above: A VT-26 T-2C over the Gulf of Mexico in June 1989. It displays the standard FS 17875 Insignia White and FS 12197 International Orange colour scheme used by training aircraft. (NARA)

Right: A VT-25 'Cougars' TA-4J in a special diamond anniversary paint scheme during events to mark the 75th anniversary of naval aviation in 1986. (NARA)

A TRAWING FOUR T-44A Pegasus on display at the Department of Defense open house air show at Andrews Air Force Base, Maryland, on 12 May 1984. TRAWING FOUR had replaced the identification letter D with G the year before. (NARA)

NAS Corpus Christi, Texas

TRAWING FOUR/TW-4 was aboard Corpus Christi. It initially used the identification letter D, switching to G by 1983. TRAWING FOUR conducted primary and intermediate training on the T-28B/C, later T-34C, and advanced multi-engined training with T-44s.

VT-27 operated fifty-seven T-28Bs and eleven T-28Cs in 1980. The T-28Cs were withdrawn by 1981, with T-28B numbers increasing, peaking at seventy-seven in 1983. T-34Cs replaced VT-27s T-28Bs by 1984, with fifty-four being operated throughout the following years, increasing to fifty-nine in 1988 and sixty-two in 1989. VT-28 and VT-31 operated the T-44As, with up to sixty operated throughout most of the decade, reducing to fifty-one by 1989.

The Station Flight operated three UH-1Ns (two from 1984) and two C-131Fs. Two UC-12s were received during 1983, and the C-131Fs were withdrawn by 1984.

Corpus Christi furnished limited support to NALF Waldron (4 miles south of Corpus Christi) and NALF Cabaniss (9 miles west of Corpus Christi). Both were supported daily by Corpus Christi tower and crash crews.

NAS Kingsville, Texas

Aboard Kingsville was TRAWING TWO/TW-2 (B) conducting intermediate and advanced strike jet training. VT-21 and VT-22 operated TA-4Js and VT-23 operated T-2Cs. In 1980 TRAWING TWO was assigned forty-nine TA-4Js and forty-seven T-2Cs. Numbers fluctuated during the decade. Fifty-eight TA-4Js and sixty-three T-2Cs were assigned during 1985; by 1989 there were seventy-one TA-4Js and fifty-five T-2Cs.

Kingsville furnished limited support to NALF Orange Grove, 30 miles north-west of Kingsville.

A T-2C of TRAWING TWO's VT-23 'Professionals' prepares to trap aboard USS *Dwight D. Eisenhower* (CVN-69) during October 1987. Landing signal officers (LSOs) are visible in the background. (NARA)

NAS Memphis, Millington, Tennessee

Aboard Memphis was Naval Air Technical Training Center (NATTC) Memphis, which provided initial and advanced aviation maintenance and support training to enlisted USN/USMC personnel. Besides maintenance, this included ordnance, air traffic control and antisubmarine warfare (ASW) equipment training. NATTC Memphis, which reported to CNTECHTRA, employed a wide range of non-flying ground instructional airframes which were utilised for this training.

The station flight operated two C-131Fs, joined by a UC-12 during 1981. The C-131Fs were retired by 1984; a second UC-12 was added during 1987.

Naval Air Reserve units aboard Memphis were Patrol Squadron VP-67 (PL), a detachment of Fleet Logistics Support Squadron VR-53 (RT) from NAS Dallas (q.v.) and NARU (Naval Air Reserve Unit) Memphis (6M). VP-67 operated nine P-3As, increasing to eleven during 1982 before settling at ten in 1983. P-3Bs were received from 1987, with eight P-3Bs and a single P-3A operated for the remainder of the decade. The VR-53 Det operated three C-118Bs, until disestablishing on 2 October 1982. In its place VR-60 (RT) was established on 3 October 1982 with two leased DC-9s. NARU Memphis operated a US-2A until 1981.

An A-4M of VMA-124 'Whistling Death' seen visiting NAS Oceana, Virginia, in August 1989. It displays Tactical Paint Scheme (TPS) camouflage. The A-4 version of TPS consisted of FS 36320 Dark Ghost Gray topsides, with FS 36375 Light Ghost Gray on most of the fin, the wing and stabiliser trailing edges and on the lower sides. The undersides were FS 36495 Light Gray. (NARA)

Also aboard Memphis was reserve Marine Attack Squadron VMA-124 (QP). This was initially assigned to the Marine Air Reserve Training Detachment (MARTD) NAS Memphis, then from 1981 to Marine Aircraft Group 42 Detachment B (MAG-42 Det B). VMA-124 operated ten A-4Es and two TA-4Js in 1980. The assigned A-4Es peaked at eighteen in 1983, before declining to fourteen by 1986; it retained its two TA-4Js throughout this period. In 1987 VMA-124 re-equipped with nineteen A-4Ms and four TA-4Fs.

Recruiting Command (NAVCRUITCOM) operated a single T-34B from Memphis. NAVCRUITCOM Recruit Quality Assurance Teams (RQATs) operated fifty-one T-34Bs to screen naval aviation candidates, and they were stationed singly across the United States, mostly at civilian airfields. These allowed recruiting officers to weed out applicants who may be unsuited to flying.

NAS Meridian, Mississippi

Aboard Meridian was TRAWING ONE/TW-1 (A) conducting intermediate and advanced strike jet training. VT-7 operated TA-4Js, while VT-9 and VT-19 operated T-2Cs. VT-9 disestablished in July 1987. VT-7 was assigned thirty-two TA-4Js in 1980. Numbers fluctuated, with forty assigned by 1983, before declining, then rising again to fifty-two by 1986. By 1988 five A-4Es joined VT-7 and fifty-five TA-4Js were operated (increasing to fifty-nine by 1989). VT-9 and VT-19 operated thirty-six T-2Cs in 1980, slowly increasing to fifty by 1985. VT-19 retained most of these T-2Cs after VT-9 disestablished, with forty-six operated by 1989.

During 1980 the station flight operated one HH-46A (retired that year), three UH-1Ns and one US-2B. In 1981 a C-1A replaced the US-2B. By 1982 the UH-1Ns were reduced to two, while the C-1A retired by 1985. A UC-12B joined the station flight in 1987.

A VT-7 'Eagles' TA-4J waits to be launched from USS *Carl Vinson* (CVN-70) on 20 April 1984. (NARA)

A TRAWING ONE T-2C about to trap aboard USS *Dwight D. Eisenhower* during October 1987; it still retains a special paint scheme celebrating the 75th anniversary of naval aviation from the year before. (NARA)

NAS Pensacola, Florida

Aboard Pensacola was TRAWING SIX/TW-6 (F) conducting intermediate and advanced strike jet training. Assigned Training Squadrons were VT-4, VT-10 and VT-86.

VT-4 conducted basic flight instruction to NFOs and some naval aviators on the E-2/C-1 special syllabus. VT-4 was equipped with fifteen TA-4Js and eighteen T-2Cs in 1980, operating nineteen of each by 1983. From 1986 only the T-2Cs remained, around nineteen being operated for the remainder of the decade.

VT-10 conducted NFO intermediate flight training. In 1980 VT-10 operated twenty-two T-2Cs and ten T-39D radar trainers. From 1982, due to a T-2C shortage, T-2Bs began to replace the former; VT-10 retired its last T-2C by 1986. T-29D numbers fluctuated around seven or eight airframes, until they were withdrawn from VT-10 in 1985. In their place, fifteen civilian contractor operated T-47As (modified, radar-equipped, Cessna Citation IIs) were introduced, these being directly assigned to TRAWING SIX from 1985. From 1985 VT-10 operated fifteen T-2Bs and also had twenty T-34Cs assigned, being so-equipped for the remainder of the decade.

A T-34C Mentor of VT-10 'Cosmic Cats' visiting NAF Washington. (NARA)

VT-86 conducted NFO advanced flight training. In 1980 VT-86 operated eight TA-4Js and eighteen T-39Ds. TA-4J numbers fluctuated between eight and eleven throughout the remainder of the decade. T-39D numbers fluctuated between seventeen and nineteen until they were withdrawn in 1985, replaced by the above mentioned T-47As.

Also under TRAWING SIX was HC-16 (BF), which provided search and rescue (SAR) in the Pensacola area and 'plane guard' cover for the training carrier USS *Lexington* (AVT-16). It was also the H-46 FRS until 1982 and the H-1 FRS throughout. In 1980 HC-16 operated thirteen HH-46As and four UH-1Ns. By 1983 they operated four and six respectively, settling out at four and seven until 1985. During 1985 five SH-3Ds replaced the HH-46As. Four SH-3Ds and six UH-1Ns were operated by 1989.

USS *Lexington* (AVT-16) was homeported at Pensacola. As a training ship that did not deploy on cruises, from 18 August 1980 *Lexington* became the first USN carrier

A VT-86 'Sabre Hawks' TA-4J taxis to the runway at NAS Pensacola on 12 May 1989. (NARA)

Civilian contractor operated T-47A Citations assigned to TRAWING SIX seen at NAS Pensacola during August 1989; note the civilian registrations. (NARA)

A HC-16 'Bullfrogs' UH-1N Iroquois performing a display during Pensacola's annual open house and air show in 1989. This UH-1N is in overall FS 16081 Engine Gray – the standard USN scheme for helicopters (apart from SH-3s) until TPS was adopted. (NARA)

A HC-16 HH-46A Sea Knight, in the standard Engine Gray scheme, seen hovering above USS *Lexington* on 24 October 1984, while providing SAR support for the training carrier. Note the loudspeaker assembly on the forward fuselage side; this was unique to HH-46A/Ds and was used to give instructions to personnel on the ground or in the water while conducting SAR missions. (NARA)

A HC-16 SH-3D winches aboard two Navy Rescue Swimmer School students during open-water exercises on the day before graduation in 1989. Those students who successfully completed the four-week course became certified search and rescue swimmers. This rather anonymous looking SH-3D features the helicopter variant of TPS which was adopted during the 1980s. This consisted of FS 36375 Light Ghost Gray fuselage sides, FS 35237 Blue Gray topsides and FS 36495 Light Gray undersides. The scheme weathered quickly, and the blotchy appearance was compounded when squadrons applied any available grey/light blue paint shade to touch up aircraft during corrosion work, as seen on the rear fuselage here. (NARA)

to have women crew members assigned. *Lexington* also had a directly assigned C-1A carrier on-board delivery (COD) aircraft until 1988; *Lexington's* C-1A made its final trap aboard *Lexington* on 27 September 1988 and retired on 30 September, the last operational reciprocating-engine aircraft in USN service.

Also aboard Pensacola was the Navy Flight Demonstration Squadron (NFDS) 'Blue Angels', which reported directly to CNATRA. In 1980 the Blue Angels operated eight A-4Fs and one TA-4J (two TA-4Js from 1984), along with their support KC-130F 'Fat Albert'. From 1987 they replaced the A-4s with eight F/A-18As and two F/A-18Bs.

The station flight operated two C-131Fs, three T-39Ds and five T-34Bs in 1980. During 1981 a sixth T-34B was added, as well as a UC-12B. During 1982 the T-34Bs reduced to five again, and a C-131G was added. By 1983 the flight operated a C-131F, a C-131G, three T-39Ds, three T-34Bs and a UC-12B. The C-131s were withdrawn during 1984. The T-34Bs were withdrawn by 1987. During 1989 a second UC-12B joined the three T-39Ds.

The NAVCRUITCOM RQAT at Pensacola had a T-34 Cadre with four T-34Bs; these were used for the usual screening, as well as to act as a reserve to backfill when other NAVCRUITCOM T-34Bs based elsewhere were being serviced.

Pensacola furnished limited support to Outlying Landing Field (OLF) Saufley Field; by 1989 this had been joined by two further satellite airfields, OLF Bronson and OLF Choctaw.

Pensacola housed a major aircraft overhaul facility, Naval Air Rework Facility (NARF) Pensacola, renamed Naval Aviation Depot (NADEP) Pensacola in 1987; it was primarily concerned with A-4, H-3, H-53 and H-60 major overhauls.

A Navy Flight Demonstration Squadron 'Blue Angels' A-4F seen at NAS Moffett Field on 3 July 1985 during the air station's annual open house and air show. An engine starter sits on the runway next to the A-4F. (NARA)

Blue Angels A-4Fs are seen executing a typically immaculate diamond take-off at Pensacola. (NARA)

A Blue Angels F/A-18A Hornet skims the runway during an air show at NAS Miramar on 19 August 1988. (NARA)

KC-130F Hercules BuNo 149806 was used as the 'Fat Albert' support aircraft for the Blue Angels from 1974 to 1987. Prior to serving with the Blue Angels it had been converted to C-130F standard by removal of its tanker equipment so that TACAMO equipment could be installed for testing. It was subsequently decided that it was not cost-effective to return 149806 to KC-130F status. After serving with the Blue Angels 149806 was transferred to VMGRT-253 at MCAS Cherry Point. (NARA)

KC-130F BuNo 149791 replaced 149806 as 'Fat Albert' with the Blue Angels from 1988. KC-130F 149791 was nicknamed *Christine* by the team, and wore this more subdued scheme. *Christine* is seen here performing the usual Fat Albert party piece of a jet-assisted take-off (JATO) at Pensacola on 12 May 1989. (NARA)

NAS Whiting Field, Florida

Aboard Whiting Field was TRAWING FIVE/TW-5 (E) conducting basic and intermediate fixed-wing training, and primary and advanced rotary-wing training.

In 1980 VT-2 and VT-3 operated 154 T-34Cs; VT-6 operated forty-eight T-28Bs. By 1983 all three squadrons operated T-34Cs, peaking with 242 T-34Cs assigned during 1984, slowly declining to 214 by 1989.

Helicopter Training Squadron HT-8 conducted primary transitional rotary-wing training (i.e. transitional between fixed-wing T-34C training and advanced rotary-wing training), while HT-18 conducted advanced rotary-wing training. In 1980 HT-8 operated thirty-six TH-57As. HT-18 operated thirty-seven TH-1Ls, thirty-two UH-1Es and five UH-1Ls; numbers peaked in late 1981 with thirty-five TH-1Ls, fifty-nine UH-1Es and five UH-1Ls, after which they slowly reduced. During the 1980s the TH-57B was introduced to augment, and later replace, the TH-57A as primary trainer, while the TH-57C was introduced to replace the various H-1 variants as advanced trainer. HT-18 retired its last H-1s during 1983. While the TH-57A was based on the Bell 206A, the TH-57B/C were based on the Bell 206B-3, with the TH-57C having more sophisticated cockpits than the TH-57B, configured with instrument flight rules (IFR) instrumentation for their advanced training role. On 7 October 1985 HT-8 and HT-18 both began teaching the full syllabus from primary through to advanced helicopter training, rather than splitting those responsibilities as previously. Thereafter the helicopters were pooled between the two squadrons, with 135 TH-57s operated by the two squadrons during October 1985. This rose to 140 (fifty-one TH-57Bs, eighty-nine TH-57Cs) during 1986, remaining at that level for the remainder of the decade.

With so many aircraft assigned to TRAWING FIVE (the largest number at any Naval Air Station), a considerable number of nearby OLFs were required to relieve the pressure of handling all of the training sorties launched each day. By 1988 Whiting Field furnished limited support to thirteen: OLF Barin, OLF Brewton, OLF Choctaw, OLF Evergreen, OLF Harold, OLF Holley, OLF Pace, OLF Santa Rosa, OLF Saufley, OLF Silverhill, OLF Spencer, OLF Summerdale and OLF Wolf.

The station flight operated two US-2Bs during 1980, replacing one with a C-1A during 1981. The other US-2B was withdrawn during 1982 and a second C-1A added during 1983, although they were withdrawn later that year, leaving the station flight without aircraft.

A plane director signals to the student flying this TRAWING FIVE TH-57C SeaRanger on approach to the deck of the USS *Lexington* during flight training on 24 October 1985. Another TH-57 approaches in the background. (NARA)

Naval Air Reserve Stations

The USN's reserve aviation units fell under Commander Naval Air Reserve, in turn under the United States Naval Reserve. The US Naval Air Reserve celebrated its 70th anniversary on 29 August 1986; by that time it consisted of fifty-two squadrons, with 357 aircraft and 34,350 full-time active duty and part-time reserve personnel. Its squadrons operated from the dedicated air stations detailed below, as well as from other air stations listed here and in the previous volume. During the 1980s, the Naval Air Reserve was going through a transition; traditionally a recipient of older, obsolescent, hand-me-down types, the reserves began to receive identical types to active frontline fleet units, including F-14As and factory-fresh F/A-18As. However, older types, long since retired from the frontline, such as the RF-8G, continued to linger in the reserves.

The Naval Air Reserve included two Reserve Carrier Air Wings (CVWRs); not assigned to a specific aircraft carrier, CVWR-20 (AF) and CVWR-30 (ND) would have respectively been assigned to Commander Naval Air Force, US Atlantic Fleet (COMNAVAIRLANT/'AirLant'), and Commander Naval Air Force, US Pacific Fleet (COMNAVAIRPAC/'AirPac'), if mobilised. The Naval Air Reserve also provided a third of all USN P-3 patrol squadrons (thirteen reserve squadrons augmenting twenty-four frontline squadrons), and all of the USN's combat SAR helicopters and heavy logistics support aircraft.

Each year reservists were expected to attend forty-eight drills (a drill weekend included four drills each of four hours) and a twelve- to fourteen-day Active Duty for Training (ACDUTRA) period. A number of full-time personnel, known as TARs (Training and Administration of the Reserve), were required to allow Naval Air Reserve units to be adequately organised, administered and trained.

A new addition to the Naval Air Reserve program during the 1980s was the creation of Squadron Augment Units (SAUs). SAUs were intended to create a pool of trained reservists, to augment fleet squadrons to wartime manning levels should the need arise. The SAUs did not have aircraft assigned, but utilised those of co-located fleet squadrons, usually those of an FRS. As they are not aircraft-equipped they are not listed in these volumes. However, to illustrate, examples included: VA-1074 (A-7 SAU) and VS-0174 (S-3 SAU) at Cecil Field; VF-1285 and VF-1485 (F-14 SAUs) and VAW-0285 (E-2 SAU) at Miramar; VP-0919 (P-3 SAU) at Moffett Field; and VP-1789 (P-3 SAU) and VA-0689 (A-6 SAU) at Whidbey Island.

NAS Atlanta, Marietta, Georgia

Naval Air Reserve squadrons aboard NAS Atlanta were Attack Squadron VA-205 with thirteen A-7Bs and VR-54 Det Atlanta (JS) with three C-118Bs. VA-205 was assigned

A VR-46 'Peach Airlines' C-118B on the flight line at Guayaquil, Ecuador, during the hemispheric naval exercise Unitas XXV on 21 June 1984; this was the USN's final C-118B deployment before the type's retirement. UNITAS XXV was silver anniversary of the naval exercise conducted between the United States and South American navies since 1959. (NARA)

to CVWR-20, and began re-equipping with A-7Es during 1984, slowly building up to twelve by 1987 and thirteen the following year. VR-54 Det Atlanta was a detachment of the NAS New Orleans-based parent squadron (q.v.); VR-54 disestablished on 28 February 1981. VR-46 (JS) was established at NAS Atlanta on 1 March 1981, taking on the three former VR-54 Det Atlanta C-118Bs, adding a fourth by 1983. The squadron's last C-118B (also the final example in USN service) was retired in February 1985; VR-46 received the first of two replacement DC-9s later that year (these ex-airline DC-9-32s purchased by the USN were designated 'DC-9' in service, rather than adopting the C-9B designation of the original purpose-built aircraft).

Marine Air Reserve squadrons aboard NAS Atlanta were Marine Observation Squadron VMO-4 (MU) with fifteen OV-10As and Marine Helicopter Attack Squadron HMA-773 (MP) with nine AH-1Js. Both squadrons were initially assigned to MAG-41 Det B, then MAG-46 Det C from 1986 and MAG-49 Det B from 1989. The strength of both squadrons fluctuated. VMO-4 operated seventeen OV-10As during much of the latter part of the decade. HMA-773 increased its AH-1J fleet to fifteen from 1987.

The station flight (7B) was assigned a UC-12B from 1983. A Naval Reserve TA-4J had also been operated by the station flight from late 1980, with a second added during 1981; they were withdrawn in 1982.

NAS Dallas, Texas

Naval Reserve squadrons aboard Dallas were Fighter Squadrons VF-201 and VF-202, and VR-53.

VF-201 and VF-202 were assigned to CVWR-20, operating F-4Ns (thirteen and fourteen respectively in 1980). They transitioned to F-4Ss (from November 1983 and February 1984 respectively), each having twelve by late 1984. The USN's final F-4 carrier landing occurred on 18 October 1986 when VF-202 F-4S Bureau Number (BuNo) 153824, flown by VF-202 XO (executive officer) commander (CDR) George Kraus, and RIO lieutenant commander (LCDR) Dave Mansfield, trapped aboard USS *America* (CV-66). VF-202 also retired the USN's last tactical (as opposed to test) F-4, when CDRs Bob Morton and Paul Siedschalg delivered F-4S BuNo 155560 to the Aerospace Maintenance and Regeneration Center (AMARC) at Davis–Monthan Air Force Base (AFB), Arizona, for storage on 14 May 1987. Transition to F-14As began when VF-201 received F-14A BuNo 158634 on 24 October 1986 at Oceana (for training under VF-101); it subsequently arrived at Dallas on 7 January 1987. VF-201's F-14A transition was complete by summer 1987, and CARQUALS were conducted aboard USS *Forrestal* (CV-59) during June. VF-202 began F-14A transition from April 1987 and conducted CARQUALS aboard USS *America* during June 1988. VF-202 was the CVWR-20 TARPS (Tactical Airborne Reconnaissance Pod System) equipped squadron, with three F-14As wired for TARPS. VF-202 participated in RAM (Reconnaissance Air Meet) '88 at Bergstrom AFB, TX, where they were placed as the top USN/USMC unit.

VR-53 (RT) operated three C-118Bs from Dallas. As noted above, it also maintained a Det at NAS Memphis. VR-59 (RY), equipped with three C-9Bs, was established on 1 October 1982, replacing VR-53, which disestablished on 2 October 1982.

Marine Reserve units aboard Dallas, and under MAG-41, were Marine Fighter/Attack Squadron VMFA-112 (MA) with fourteen F-4Ns and Marine Heavy Helicopter Squadron HMH-777 (QM) with six CH-53As. VMFA-112 transitioned to F-4Js from

A VF-201 'Hunters' F-4S Phantom II, painted in the toned-down Tactical Paint Scheme, on the deck of USS *Dwight D. Eisenhower* while deployed aboard for CARQUALs with CVWR-20 on 15 September 1985. A HS-75 'Emerald Knights' SH-3D is in the background. (NARA)

July 1983 and then F-4Ss from February 1985. HMH-777 disestablished during 1980, its assets then forming HMH-772 Det B (MT). HMH-772's HQ was aboard NAS Willow Grove (q.v.). HMH-772 Det B operated up to seven CH-53As for the remainder of the decade.

Dallas' station flight (7D) operated a US-2A and a US-2B, both replaced by a UC-12B during 1980. Two UC-12Bs were briefly operated during 1982, reverting to just one for the remainder of the decade. Also directly assigned to the station (and also using the station's 7D identification tailcode) was the Operational Maintenance Department (OMD), which was perhaps the USN's least known adversary unit, after adding that role to its other duties during the 1980s. OMD operated a handful of A-4s, mainly in support of the Naval Air Reserve. OMD was usually assigned around three TA-4Js (periodically fluctuating between one and four); from 1987 A-4Ms began to replace the TA-4Js, with three A-4Ms operated by 1988–89. OMD's A-4s were painted in the grey Tactical Paint Scheme (TPS).

NAF Detroit, Mt. Clemens, Michigan

Naval Reserve units aboard Naval Air Facility (NAF) Detroit were VP-93 (LH) and VR-52 Det Detroit (JT). VP-93 operated nine P-3As, replaced with P-3Bs from 1981. The Detroit detachment of Willow Grove's VR-52 (q.v.) operated three C-118Bs (four from 1981). On 1 October 1982 VR-62 (JW), operating two DC-9s, was established to replace VR-52 Det Detroit.

Detroit's station flight (7Y) operated a US-2A until 1980. From 1983 a UC-12B was operated.

NAS Glenview, Illinois

Naval Reserve units aboard Glenview were VP-60 (LS), VP-90 (LX) and VR-51 (RV).

VP-60 and VP-90 transitioned from P-3As to P-3Bs during 1980 and 1981 respectively, although VP-90 retained a single P-3A until late 1982. The number of P-3s assigned to both squadrons fluctuated throughout the decade, between seven and eleven, although generally around nine were assigned to each. By 1984 both squadrons were operating P-3B TACNAVMODs, which were P-3Bs updated with P-3C systems through the Tactical-Navigation Modernization programme. TACNAVMOD Block 1 added AQA-79(V)5 acoustic DIFAR (Directional Acoustic Frequency Analysis and Recording System) with a new sonobuoy receiver, sonodata processor and tape recorder set. The ASN-72 INS (inertial navigation system) with backup OMEGA radio navigation was also added. New displays were added for the pilots and TACCO (Tactical Coordinator). By 1987 both squadrons each operated eight P-3B TACNAVMODs and one P-3A, the P-3As presumably used as air crew trainers.

VR-51 operated four C-118Bs; VR-51 also had a permanent detachment at NAS Whidbey Island with another four C-118Bs until the det disestablished during 1982. During 1983 VR-51 re-equipped with its first C-9B, with two on strength from late 1984.

Two Marine Air Reserve units were aboard Glenview, Marine Aerial Refueler Transport Squadron VMGR-234 (QH) and Marine Light Helicopter Squadron HML-776 (QL). VMGR-234 operated seven KC-130Fs. During 1984 four KC-130Ts

Seen on display at NAS Pensacola during the celebration of the 75th anniversary of naval aviation in 1986 are, from top to bottom, a VMGR-234 'Thundering Herd' KC-130F from NAS Glenview, a VP-44 'Golden Pelicans' P-3C Orion from NAS Brunswick and a VP-94 'Crawfishers' P-3B TACNAVMOD from NAS New Orleans. (NARA)

joined the KC-130Fs; by 1986 VMGR-234 operated seven KC-130Fs and eight KC-130Ts. HML-776 operated eight UH-1Es, later dropping to six before stabilising at seven by 1982; HML-776 transitioned to seven UH-1Ns during 1987.

Glenview's station flight operated two US-2Bs, replaced by a UC-12B by 1981 (briefly operating two UC-12Bs during 1982, before returning to just one).

NAVCRUITCOM operated a T-34B from Glenview from 1980 onwards.

NAS New Orleans, Louisiana

Naval Reserve units aboard New Orleans were VA-204, VP-94 (LZ) and VR-54 (JS).

VA-204, assigned to CVWR-20, operated twelve A-7Bs, increasing to fourteen by 1987. In 1989 VA-204 transitioned to twelve A-7Es.

VP-94 operated P-3As, fluctuating between eight and ten. VP-94 began transitioning to P-3B TACNAVMODs during 1984, having ten by 1987.

VR-54 had four C-118Bs aboard New Orleans until it disestablished on 28 February 1981; as noted above, VR-54 also had a permanent three-C-118B detachment at Atlanta.

The pilot of this VA-204 'River Rattlers' A-7B Corsair II pushes his head firmly against the headrest of his ejection seat in preparation for a catapult launch from USS *Dwight D. Eisenhower* on 15 September 1985. VA-204 was deployed aboard the 'Ike' for CARQUALs with CVWR-20. This A-7B displays the original scheme of FS 16440 Light Gull Gray topsides and gloss FS 17875 Insignia White undersides. (NARA)

The original UC-12B operated by NAS New Orleans' station flight, BuNo 161186, seen soon after delivery in 1979. (NARA)

The Marine Reserve's HML-767 (MM), under MAG-46 Det B, was aboard New Orleans with UH-1Ns (fluctuating around fifteen). MAG-46 Det B also had a UC-12B directly assigned briefly during 1982, and later two UC-12Bs assigned from 1985 onwards.

The station flight (7X) at New Orleans was assigned two CT-39Gs, one C-131F, three TA-4Js and one UC-12B in 1980. The TA-4Js (which retained the white/orange training colour scheme) were withdrawn by early 1981. A second UC-12B was added by early 1983. The C-131F was withdrawn by early 1985, while one of the UC-12Bs was withdrawn later in 1985. From 1987 the two CT-39Gs were directly controlled by COMNAVAIRESFOR (Commander, Naval Air Reserve Force) Flight Operations. A second UC-12B was once again added in 1989.

NAS South Weymouth, Massachusetts

Naval Reserve units aboard South Weymouth were Helicopter Anti-Submarine Squadron HS-74 (NW) and VP-92 (LY). HS-74 operated seven or eight SH-3Ds until 1984 when it was reduced to four. In January 1985 HS-74 became Helicopter Anti-Submarine Squadron, Light HSL-74, retaining the NW identification code common to Helicopter Wing Reserve (HELWINGRES) squadrons; it re-equipped with eight SH-2Fs. VP-92 operated nine P-3As, peaking at ten during 1983. VP-92 transitioned to seven P-3Bs during 1984, peaking at ten by 1986, settling on nine by 1988.

Marine Reserve squadrons aboard South Weymouth were HML-771 (QK) and VMA-322 (QR), both under MAG-49 Det A. HML-771 (QK) operated seven UH-1Es, replaced by twelve UH-1Ns from 1981, reduced to eight UH-1Ns from 1987. VMA-322 operated twelve A-4Es and two TA-4Js (just one from 1982). During 1983 VMA-322 transitioned to thirteen A-4Ms and added a second TA-4J once again. By 1985 VMA-322 operated fifteen A-4Ms and two TA-4Js, reducing respectively to fourteen and one by 1987. During 1989 the TA-4J was replaced by a TA-4F.

The station flight (7Z) operated a UC-12B from 1981.

Above: A HS-74 'Minutemen' SH-3D seen aboard the Thomaston-class dock-landing ship USS *Plymouth Rock* (LSD-29). (NARA)

Right: A VMA-332 A-4M on the flight line at NAS Dallas while visiting on 1 February 1988. (NARA)

NAF Washington, DC

NAF Washington was located within Andrews AFB. Naval Reserve units aboard Washington at the outset of the decade were VR-52 Det Washington (JT) and Light Photographic Squadrons VFP-206 and VFP-306.

The Washington detachment of Willow Grove's VR-52 (q.v.) operated three C-131Hs. VR-52 Det Washington was replaced by VR-48 (JR), which was established on 1 October 1980, taking over the three C-131Hs, reduced to two during 1986.

VFP-206 and VFP-306 were assigned to CVWR-20 (AF) and CVWR-30 (ND) respectively, each operating four RF-8Gs, increasing to five each during 1982. VFP-306 disestablished on 1 October 1984; VFP-206, the final USN Crusader unit, disestablished on 29 March 1987.

A VR-48 C-131F Samaritan in flight off the coast of Florida during 1983. (NARA)

Flight deck crewmen perform pre-flight checks on a VFP-206 'Hawkeyes' RF-8G Crusader aboard the USS *Dwight D. Eisenhower* on 15 September 1985, while deployed for CARQUALs with CVWR-20. This RF-8G features an overall FS 16440 Light Gull Gray scheme. This replaced the original scheme of FS 16440 Light Gull Gray topsides and gloss FS 17875 Insignia White undersides on most F-4s and F-14s, as well as RF-8Gs, around the start of the 1980s. This was an interim scheme to reduce aircraft visibility pending the adoption of TPS. (NARA)

The Naval Reserve squadron VP-68 (LW) relocated from NAS Patuxent River to NAF Washington on 1 April 1985. VP-68 was transitioning from P-3As to P-3B TACNAVMODs as it relocated, and completed the transition in November 1985, with eight airframes.

The Marine Reserve's VMFA-321 (MG) was assigned to MAG-41, from 2 June 1980 to MAG-41 Det A. VMFA-321 operated twelve F-4Ns, transitioning to twelve F-4Ss during late 1984.

A VFP-206 RF-8G about to catch the wire aboard *Ike* on 19 September 1985, the final day of CVWR-20's 1985 CARQUALs. A similar CVWR-20 CARQUAL deployment aboard USS *America* (CV-66) thirteen months later would see the final carrier deployment by USN Phantom IIs and Crusaders. On 18 October 1986 VF-202 F-4S BuNo 153824, flown by VF-202 XO CDR George Kraus and RIO LCDR Dave Mansfield, made the final F-4 trap; a few minutes later the final Crusader trap was conducted by VFP-206's LCDR Barry Gabler in RF-8G BuNo 145633. Gabler and 145633 also made the final Crusader catapult launch later that day, a short time after the final F-4 launch. Therefore, the F-8 outlived the F-4 in carrier service, if only by a matter of minutes! (NARA)

Two VFP-206 RF-8Gs in formation over Texas on 1 November 1986, during a mission from Bergstrom AFB while participating in the USAF Tactical Air Command's Reconnaissance Air Meet '86 competition. The nearest aircraft retains the interim overall FS 16440 Light Gull Gray, while the rear aircraft is in the new TPS scheme, which began to be adopted by RF-8Gs from February 1984. (NARA)

Two TPS camouflaged VFP-206 RF-8Gs on the flight line at NAF Washington on 20 March 1987, just over a week before the unit's disestablishment on 29 March 1987. (NARA)

Anonymous looking P-3B TACNAVMODs of VP-68 'Blackhawks' while making an Active Duty for Training (ACDUTRA) deployment to Naval Station Rota, Spain, during May 1989. While the background aircraft retains the original scheme of Insignia White topsides and Light Gull Gray undersides, the foreground aircraft has received the new TPS finish. (NARA)

A VMFA-321 'Hells Angels' F-4S seen on 17 July 1987. During the late 1980s some USMC F-4s, including this aircraft, had their Tactical Paint Scheme modified with the addition of FS 36118 Medium Gunship Gray topsides – this was not a standard TPS colour. This F-4S (BuNo 153887) was withdrawn from use in July 1991, and later converted into a QF-4S drone; it was expended in a missile test on 18 July 2001. (NARA)

NAF Washington station flight UC-12B BuNo 161498 on display at the Department of Defense open house air show at Andrews AFB (which NAF Washington was located within) on 12 May 1984. (NARA)

One of two immaculate COMFLELOGSUPWINGDET TA-3B Skywarriors seen on 8 May 1987, a short time before they were replaced as high-speed transports for the Chief of Naval Operations by two C-20Ds. (NARA)

The station flight (7N) operated one C-131F until 1980; from 1981 a UC-12B was assigned.

Also aboard Washington was COMRESTACSUPWING DET (Commander Reserve Tactical Support Wing Detachment), which operated three C-131Fs and a TA-3B for VIP transportation; the TA-3B acted as a high speed transport for the Chief of Naval Operations (CNO). During 1981 the C-131Fs were replaced by two CT-39Gs. A second TA-3B was added during 1982. COMRESTACSUPPWING DET became COMFLELOGSUPWINGDET (Commander Fleet Logistics Support Wing – CFLSW – Detachment) from 1984. Both TA-3Bs were replaced by two C-20Ds during 1987.

The Marine Aircraft Support Detachment (MASD) operated VIP aircraft from Washington on behalf of Headquarters USMC. It did not originally fall under any of the Marine Air Wings; instead it was attached directly to Headquarters Battalion, Headquarters, US Marine Corps (HQBN HQMC). In 1980 MASD operated a VC-118B and a VC-131G, adding a UC-12B later during 1980, and a second during 1981. The VC-118B and VC-131G were withdrawn by 1982. On 3 April 1982, MASD was commissioned into the 4th Marine Air Wing as a reserve detachment (tailcode 5A), retaining its two UC-12Bs for the remainder of the decade.

NAS Willow Grove, Pennsylvania

Naval Reserve units aboard Willow Grove were HS-75 (NW), VP-64 (LU), VP-66 (LV) and VR-52 (JT).

HS-75 operated SH-3Ds, fluctuating between six and nine; it replaced NAS North Island's HS-84 within CVWR-20 around 1984. During 1985 HS-75 relocated to NAS Jacksonville, Florida. In its place HSL-94 (NW) was established at Willow Grove on 1 October 1985 operating SH-2Fs, building up to eight aircraft by 1987.

VP-64 and VP-66 each operated nine P-3As in 1980, with numbers fluctuating during the decade, both having ten by 1989.

VR-52 operated four C-118Bs from Willow Grove in 1980, with numbers fluctuating over the following years. As mentioned above, VR-52 also maintained two dets: VR-52 Det Detroit with three C-118Bs until 1982, and VR-52 Det Washington

A VP-64 'Condors' P-3A seen on the Naval Air Reserve flight line at NAS Norfolk, Virginia, while visiting there on 17 January 1984. Visible in the background are locally based EA-6A Intruders of VAQ-209 and an E-2 Hawkeye of VAW-78. (NARA)

A VR-52 'Taskmasters' DC-9 seen at NAS Oceana, Virginia, during 1989. This DC-9-32CF had served with Overseas National Airways, Air Canada, Southern Airways and Republic Airlines before being taken on by the USN in 1984 as BuNo 163036 and assigned to VR-52, who named it *City of Philadelphia*. While the USN's original purpose-built DC-9 variants were designated 'C-9B Skytrain II', the ex-airline DC-9s retained the 'DC-9' designation in USN service. (NARA)

with three C-131Hs until 1980. VR-52 received two DC-9s by 1986 to replace its C-118Bs at Willow Grove.

Marine Reserve units aboard Willow Grove were under MAG-49.

HMH-772 (MT) operated up to seven CH-53As from Willow Grove. HMH-772 also had two CH-53A dets from 1980 onwards, Det A at Alameda and Det B at Dallas. Dets A and B had replaced reserve squadrons disestablished during 1980, HMH-769 and HMH-777 respectively, absorbing their personnel and equipment. As two-thirds of HMH-772's strength was located away from Willow Grove, the element of the squadron at its home station was known as HMH-772(-).

VMA-131 (QG) operated eleven A-4Es and two TA-4Js in 1980, with two TA-4Fs replacing the TA-4Js later that year. Strength peaked during 1983–84 when seventeen A-4Es and one TA-4F were operated. During 1987 VMA-131 re-equipped with fourteen A-4Ms and four TA-4Js.

Another MAG-49 Marine Reserve squadron should be mentioned, although not located aboard Willow Grove: VMGR-452 (NY) was uniquely established at Stewart Air National Guard Base (ANGB), New York, a non-naval aviation facility, on 9 September 1988 under MAG-49, operating KC-130Ts.

Willow Grove's station flight (7W) operated a US-2B, replaced by a UC-12B during 1980.

Naval Aviation Research, Development and Test Stations

Naval Air Systems Command (NAVAIRSYSCOM, 'NAVAIR') provided (and continues to provide) full life-cycle support of USN and USMC aircraft, weapons and systems. This included overseeing research, design, development, systems engineering, acquisition, test and evaluation, training, logistics, repair and modification, and in-service support.

Naval Weapons Center (NAVWPNCEN) China Lake, California

Responsible for research, development and test of naval weapons, the expansive Naval Weapons Center China Lake range complex was primarily focused on naval air warfare. NAVWPNCEN dealt with conventional and nuclear, guided and unguided, powered and free-fall ordnance. It therefore incorporated weapons ranges, which included surplus aircraft as targets, and operated a large mixed fleet of aircraft and target drones from Armitage Field within the complex. NAVWPNCEN was controlled by NAVAIR.

In 1980 NAVWPNCEN (featuring NWC CHINA LAKE tail markings in lieu of a tailcode) operated single examples of A-4F, NA-4F, A-4M, NA-7C, C-131, C-117D, YF-4J, T-39D and OV-10A, two each TA-4J, A-7C, TA-7C, UH-1N, T-38A and RU-9D (Aero Commanders used for various project support duties), and three each A-6E and A-7E. NAVWPNCEN also operated six QF-86H (ex-Air National Guard airframes), nineteen QF-86F (ex-Japanese Air Self Defense Force airframes) and five QT-38A drones. By 1985 NAVWPNCEN operated single examples of NA-3B, A-7C, YF-4J, T-39D, T-38A and UC-8A (DHC-5 Buffalo), two each TA-4J, TA-7C and UH-1N, three each A-4M and A-7E, and four each A-6E and F/A-18. It also operated one each QF-4B and QT-38A and six QF-86F drones. By 1989 NAVWPNCEN operated single examples of NA-3B, A-4F, TA-4J, A-7C, YF-4J, T-39D and UC-8A, two each A-4M, TA-7C, AV-8B, TH-1L and Mitsubishi MU-2L, three each A-6E and A-7E, four HH-1Ks and seven F/A-18s. It also operated four QF-4N and six QF-86F drones.

Also stationed aboard Armitage Field/China Lake was Air Test and Evaluation Squadron VX-5 (XE) assigned to AirPac; VX-5 developed ordnance delivery tactics and techniques. In 1980 VX-5 operated two TA-7Cs, six A-7Es, five A-6Es, three A-4Ms, one OA-4M, one TA-4J, one C-1A, one AH-1J and one AH-1T. During 1981 a UH-1N and two AV-8A/Cs were briefly assigned; two F/A-18As and a TF-18A (later redesignated F/A-18B) were assigned from 1982. By 1983 one TA-7C, five A-7Es, four A-6Es, two A-4Ms, one TA-4J, two F/A-18As and four TF-18As were assigned. During 1984 the TA-7C was withdrawn, a fifth A-6E was added, the F/A-18A fleet increased to four and the TF-18As withdrawn, while two AV-8Bs, an OV-10A and an AH-1J were assigned. Numbers of assigned aircraft

A Naval Weapons Center A-7E seen loaded with an AGM-123 Skipper II rocket-powered laser-guided bomb (LGB) ahead of a September 1981 test. Existing, unpowered, Paveway II LGBs lacked stand-off range, especially when dropped from low level; Skipper II, developed in-house by NAVWPNCEN, was intended to remedy this. It mated a GBU-16A/B Paveway II LGB (itself consisting of a Mk 83 1,000-lb bomb with a Paveway laser guidance kit) to an Aerojet Mk 78 rocket motor salvaged from obsolete AGM-45B Shrike missiles. Although crude, it was effective and only a quarter of the cost of the USAF's Paveway III series of extended range unpowered LGBs that were developed to meet a similar requirement. Skipper II's theoretical 34-mile (55-km) range was usually limited to about 15 miles (25 km) by the range of the laser designator, normally mounted on the launching aircraft. After development, Emerson Electric was awarded a contract for full-scale production of 2,500 AGM-123A Skipper IIs in March 1985, primarily for use by A-6Es in the anti-shipping role. Skipper II was first used in anger during Operation *Praying Mantis* on 18 April 1988 when VA-95 A-6Es attacked the Iranian frigate *Sahand*. (NARA)

A Naval Weapons Center A-7E flown by LCDR R. Kapernick loaded with inert training Mk 82 500-lb bombs over the Coso Bombing Range, which formed part of the Naval Weapons Center, on 1 November 1981. (NARA)

continued to fluctuate, with a Cessna 206, one OV-10D, an AH-1T and two TA-7Cs added during 1987. By 1988 three A-7Es, two TA-7Cs, one AH-1J, one AH-1W, two AV-8Bs, three A-6Es, two TA-4Js, five F/A-18A/Cs, one Cessna 207 and one OV-10 assigned. During 1989 the AV-8Bs were reduced to one and the F/A-18s reduced to four, an EA-6B and Cessna 182 were added, and the OV-10 withdrawn.

China Lake also routinely supported training deployments by USN and USMC squadrons.

A VX-5 'Vampires' AV-8C Harrier at China Lake on 15 September 1981 armed with an ATM-122, the training version of the AGM-122A Sidearm. The Sidearm was a lightweight anti-radiation missile conceived and developed at China Lake, and produced by remanufacturing redundant AIM-9C Sidewinder air-to-air missiles. Intended for carriage by USMC AV-8s and AH-1s, Sidearm was first tested in 1981. Motorola was awarded a contract to convert AIM-9Cs to AGM-122A standard in 1984, with around 700 produced between 1986 and 1990. (NARA)

VX-5 AH-1T Improved SeaCobra BuNo 159228 carrying an ATM-122 at China Lake on 16 October 1981. BuNo 159228 was built as the last-but-one AH-1J SeaCobra, but was converted into the first AH-1T before delivery in 1976; much later, it was further converted into an AH-1W SuperCobra. The first thirty-three AH-1Ts lacked TOW missile capability and were delivered without the nose-mounted M65 Telescopic Sight Unit (TSU), therefore retaining the AH-1J's pointed nose as seen here; TOW capability and the M65 TSU was later retrofitted to surviving early AH-1Ts. (NARA)

A VX-5 A-7E carrying two live AGM-65E Mavericks, about to launch from USS *Constellation* (CV-64) in the Pacific Ocean on 9 August 1988. The AGM-65E was a unique semi-active laser-guided Maverick variant, primarily used by the USMC to allow Marines to self-designate ground targets for close air support. Other Maverick variants utilised either electro-optical (TV) or imaging infrared guidance. (NARA)

Left: A VX-5 F/A-18C carrying an AGM-88 HARM (High-speed Anti-Radiation Missile) during 1988. A blue CATM-9L (a captive training AIM-9L Sidewinder) is on the wingtip. (NARA)

Below: A VX-5 AV-8B Harrier II hovering during a display at the Point Mugu air show in 1989. (NARA)

Naval Air Engineering Center (NAVAIRENGCEN) Lakehurst, New Jersey

NAVAIRENGCEN Lakehurst, under NAVAIR, conducted research and development of aircraft carrier launch and recovery equipment and naval aviation support equipment.

In 1980 NAVAIRENGCEN was assigned an A-7B and an NTA-4F, both for catapult testing, as well as a U-3A and a US-2B. A UH-1M was added during 1980. Two U-8Gs replaced the U-3A and US-2B during 1981. The UH-1M was replaced by a TH-1L during 1983. The A-7B and NTA-4F were replaced by a TA-7C by 1986, which itself was withdrawn by 1988. The two U-8Gs were withdrawn by 1989, leaving just the TH-1L.

Also aboard Lakehurst was NATTC Lakehurst, which trained enlisted personnel in handling aviation fuel, and catapult and arrestor gear operation. The latter training was conducted in Lakehurst's huge Hanger 1, originally constructed for airships in 1921. Within Hanger 1 was the Carrier Aircraft Launch and Support System/Equipment Simulator (CALASSES), a 119-metre-long (390-ft) mock carrier deck elevated above the floor. CALASSES included all the usual carrier deck features, such as the control tower 'island', emergency barricade, 'cross deck pendant' (arrestor wires), catapult tracks and Fresnel lens 'meatball' visual landing aid. It was large enough to allow for real airframes (including a T-34B and an A-4) to be maneuvered 'on deck'. NATTC Lakehurst reported to CNTECHTRA and was assigned a C-1A to provide support. This C-1A (BuNo 136792) was unusual as it had originally been modified to act as the aerodynamic prototype of the E-1 Tracer, with large radome above the fuselage and twin-tails, although lacking the associated electronics. It had been returned to C-1A configuration by 1970, including removal of the radome, but retained the twin-tails. This uniquely configured C-1A remained assigned to NATTC Lakehurst until it was struck off charge on 3 February 1983. A second C-1A was added by 1982, and two C-1As (another airframe replacing twin-tailed 136792) were operated by NATTC Lakehurst until 1986.

NAS Patuxent River, Maryland

The Naval Air Test Center (NATC), under NAVAIR, aboard Patuxent River (or 'Pax River') was divided into several directorates. The Strike Aircraft Test Directorate tested fixed wing combat and some training aircraft. The Rotary Wing Aircraft Test Directorate tested rotary wing (and later tilt-rotor) aircraft. The Antisubmarine Aircraft Test Directorate tested ASW, airborne early warning (AEW), transport, ballistic-missile submarine (SSBN) communications ('Take Charge And Move Out' – TACAMO), Electronic Intelligence/Signals Intelligence (ELINT/SIGINT) and some training types. To better reflect its mission, Antisubmarine Aircraft Test Directorate became the Force Warfare Aircraft Test Directorate in June 1986. The Systems Engineering Test Directorate tested everything from electronic warfare systems to computers, ejections seats and electrical systems. The Technical Support Directorate (renamed the Range Directorate in 1985) provided fixed and mobile targets, as well as handling the instrumentation of aircraft to gather flight test data. The Computer Sciences Directorate processed the flight test data, as well as providing wider computer support. Also part of NATC was the US Naval Test Pilot School (USNTPS), which not only trained test pilots for the USN and USMC, but as the only US military test pilot school providing rotary-wing aircraft instruction, USNTPS also acted as the primary test pilot school for the US Army. Other students came from the USAF, the UK and France on an exchange basis. NATC replaced the 7T tailcode with the SD tailcode in 1986.

NATC's large and varied fleet was in a constant state of flux. In April 1980, NATC operated 104 aircraft, as follows:

Two KA-3Bs, eight TA-4Js, one NA-4M, two A-4Ms, two A-6Es, two A-7Cs, three TA-7Cs, one NA-7E, six A-7Es, one AV-8A and one AV-8C. Eight F-4Js, five F-14As, nine F/A-18As and two TF-18As (these Hornets were the first eleven build and were bailed to McDonnell Douglas while undergoing developmental test and evaluation [DT&E]). Two E-2Cs, one P-3B, two P-3Cs, three S-3As, one EC-130G, one UC-12B, eight T-2Cs, five T-38As, one T-39D, one NU-1B (Otter), one U-6A (Beaver) and two X-26A sailplanes. Four AH-1Gs (not a usual naval type, but these were passed to the USN from the USMC who had operated AH-1Gs pending receiving their own dedicated twin-engined AH-1J variant), three AH-1Ts, two UH-1Ns, one SH-2F, one SH-3D, two SH-3Hs, one CH-46A, one NCH-46A, one CH-46E and one CH-53D. There were also three OV-1Bs and three OH-58As on loan from the US Army to support USNTPS.

By October 1985 NATC operated 102 aircraft: Six TA-4Js, three A-4Ms, one NA-4M, three A-6Es, one TA-7C, four A-7Es, one NA-7E, three AV-8Bs and one AV-8C. Three F-4Js, one F-4S, five F-14As, six F/A-18As and four F/A-18Bs. Two C-2As, one E-2B, one E-2C, one P-3B, two P-3Cs, three S-3As, one EC-130G and one UC-880 (Convair 880). Six T-2Cs, two T-34Cs, five T-38As, one T-44A, one NU-1B, one U-6A and one X-26A. One AH-1J, one AH-1T, one TH-1L, one UH-1N, two SH-2Fs, one SH-3H, two CH-46As, one NCH-46A, one HH-46A, one CH-46D, two CH-46Es, one CH-53A, two CH-53Es, one TH-57C and three JSH-60Bs. NATC was also loaning four OH-58As, three UH-60As and three OV-1Bs from the US Army.

An NATC Strike Aircraft Test Directorate F-14A Tomcat taking off from a nine-degree ski jump during feasibility tests at Patuxent River in September 1982. The F-14A conducted twenty-eight ski-jump launches during the trials, which also involved the AV-8, F/A-18 and T-2, and explored possible use of ski jumps on carriers instead of catapults. The USN did not go on to adopt ski jumps. This F-14A displays NATC's original 7T tailcode, and high-visibility International Orange panels, typical of NATC aircraft. (NARA)

Above: An NATC Antisubmarine Aircraft Test Directorate S-3A Viking on public display during Pax River's open house Expo '83 in August 1983. (NARA)

Right: An NATC OV-10A Bronco on display during Expo '83. (NARA)

Below: The US Naval Test Pilot School (USNTPS) NU-1B Otter on display during Expo '83. (NARA)

The USNTPS U-6A Beaver on display during Expo '83. Test pilot training requires a broad range of very varied types which students train on and assess as part of their schooling. (NARA)

Above: A USNTPS T-38A Talon on display during Expo '83. In the background right a USNTPS T-2C is visible, while background left a NATC Rotary Wing Aircraft Test Directorate SH-3 can be seen. (NARA)

Below: The USNTPS X-26A Frigate sailplane on display at Pax River's 1984 open house air show. (NARA)

The UC-880 of NATC's Force Warfare Aircraft Test Directorate, seen refuelling a TA-4J on 3 September 1986; until that June the directorate had been named the Antisubmarine Aircraft Test Directorate. The UC-880 had earlier supported the initial F/A-18 in-flight refuelling trials. NATC's single UC-880 was not just employed for in-flight refuelling with its centre-mounted hose drogue unit, but on a wide range of tasks, including supporting the development of the Tomahawk cruise missile, surveillance, and command and control. (NARA)

NATC Strike Aircraft Test Directorate aircraft operating from USS *Abraham Lincoln* (CVN-72) on 3 December 1989, during flight deck certification of the new aircraft carrier in the Atlantic. *Abe* had been commissioned three weeks earlier, on 11 November 1989. An F/A-18D has just trapped aboard, while two A-7Es are visible in the foreground. Partially visible in the right background is an F-14A. The aircraft display the SD tailcode, which NATC had adopted in 1986. (NARA)

By October 1989 NATC operated 126 aircraft: Four TA-4Js, four A-4Ms, four A-6Es, three EA-6Bs, nine TA-7Cs, three A-7Es, three AV-8Bs and one TAV-8B. Ten F-14As, six F/A-18As, four F/A-18Bs, one F/A-18C and one F/A-18D. One OV-10D, one C-2A, three E-2Cs, two P-3Bs, three P-3Cs, two S-3As, one S-3B and one UC-880. Six T-2Cs, one T-34C, one NT-34C, six T-38As, one T-39D, one NU-1B, one U-6A and one X-26A. One AH-1J, one AH-1T, two AH-1Ws, one UH-1N, two SH-2Fs, one HH-3A, one VH-3A, two SH-3Hs, one CH-46E, one CH-53A, one CH-53D, one CH-53E, one JMH-53E, two TH-57As, seven SH-60Bs, two SH-60Fs and two HH-60Hs. NATC was also loaning four OH-58As, three UH-60As and two U-21As from the US Army, and three HH-65As from the US Coast Guard.

Other squadrons aboard Patuxent River were Fleet Air Reconnaissance Squadron VQ-4 (HL), VX-1 (JA), and Oceanographic Development Squadron VXN-8 (JB).

VQ-4, assigned to Tactical Support Wing One (TACSUPWING ONE), operated two EC-130Gs and eight EC-130Qs in the TACAMO role, maintaining communications links between the National Command Authority and submerged USN ballistic missile submarines (SSBNs), along with one KC-130F trainer/support aircraft. By late 1982 VQ-4 operated five EC-130Qs (still with two EC-130Gs and the KC-130F), remaining so-equipped until 1986 when a sixth EC-130Q was added and the KC-130F withdrawn. By 1987 a seventh EC-130Q was added and the EC-130Gs withdrawn, however one trainer/support TC-130G (a former EC-130G with TACAMO equipment removed) was added. The EC-130Q's replacement in the TACAMO role was the E-6A. TACAMO equipment was removed from EC-130Qs and installed on the E-6As; the former EC-130Qs were then operated as TC-130Q trainer/support aircraft. Consequently a TC-130Q joined VQ-4's seven EC-130Qs and single TC-130G in 1987; a second TC-130Q was added in 1989. Meanwhile, during 1989 the E-6A entered service with VQ-4's sister squadron, VQ-3 at NAS Barbers Point, Hawaii. However, VQ-4 would not receive its first replacement E-6A until January 1991.

VX-1, assigned to Sea Based Anti-Submarine Warfare Wings Atlantic (SEABASEDASWWINGSLANT), conducted ASW test and evaluation. In 1980 VX-1 was assigned one EP-3A, five P-3Cs, one SH-2F, four SH-3Hs and three S-3As. Aircraft assignments fluctuated during the decade. By late 1984 VX-1 operated three P-3Cs, two SH-2Fs, one SH-3D, one SH-3H, two SH-60Bs (which joined the squadron that

A VQ-4 'Shadows' EC-130Q in flight on 5 November 1984. (NARA)

year) and one S-3A; the EP-3A had been withdrawn earlier that year. In 1989 VX-1 was reassigned from SEABASEDASWWINGSLANT to Patrol Wings Atlantic (PATWINGSLANT). By October 1989 VX-1 was assigned four P-3Cs, two SH-2Fs, two SH-3Hs, three SH-60Bs, one S-3A and two S-3Bs.

VXN-8, assigned to TACSUPWING ONE, was the only aviation squadron in the US military (and indeed the western world) dedicated to airborne oceanographic and geomagnetic surveys. VXN-8 was assigned three specific projects. The oldest was Project Magnet, assigned since 1951, which involved collecting worldwide magnetic data required for ASW and other scientific purposes; up-to-date information was constantly collected and rapidly disseminated. Project Outpost Seascan studied the thermal and acoustic characteristics of oceans for ASW purposes. Finally, Project Birdseye involved polar research, with approximately nine missions per year over arctic sea ice. This sought to improve ice observation techniques, refine forecasting techniques, collect data for military Arctic operations, and support USN submarine under-ice operations.

To support these projects, VXN-8's fleet in 1980 consisted of two RP-3As and two RP-3Ds. One RP-3A was withdrawn on 7 February 1981. On 14 February 1982 a P-3A was assigned, and a second on 19 July 1982; one of the P-3As was transferred out of VXN-8 (to VAQ-33) on 19 April 1983. An additional RP-3D was added on 31 August 1984, VXN-8 then operating one RP-3A, three RP-3Ds and one P-3A. On 15 March 1985 a second P-3A was once again assigned. On 16 April 1985 one of VXN-8's RP-3Ds and one of its P-3As were both redesignated as UP-3As, giving a fleet of one RP-3A, two RP-3Ds, two UP-3As and one P-3A. VXN-8's remaining P-3A was transferred to VP-MAU Brunswick in January 1987. Finally, a third UP-3A was assigned to VXN-8 during April 1988, giving a fleet of one RP-3A, two RP-3Ds and three UP-3As.

Also aboard Patuxent River was the Naval Research Laboratory (NRL) Flight Support Detachment (NRLFLTSUPDET), supporting NRL airborne research projects

RP-3D BuNo 153443 'El Coyote' of VXN-8 'World Travellers' on display during the 1987 Pax River open house. BuNo 153443 had earlier served as the YP-3C prototype from 1968. It went on to have a test career with NATC, NADC and VX-1, before joining VXN-8 on 31 August 1984, modified and redesignated as an RP-3D dual-mission Project Outpost Seascan and Project Birdseye mission aircraft. (NARA)

(under Director, NRL, Washington, DC). In 1980 NRLFLTSUPDET operated one EP-3A, one RP-3A, one EP-3B and one S-2D. During 1981 the S-2D was replaced by a P-3A. An F-14A was briefly added during 1983. On 16 April 1985 the P-3A was redesignated as a UP-3A, giving a fleet of one each EP-3A, RP-3A, UP-3A and EP-3B, which remained constant for the remainder of the decade.

NAS Norfolk's Fleet Composite Squadron VC-6 (JG), under TACSUPWING ONE, established VC-6 RPV Det 1 at Patuxent River during July 1986 to operate the Pioneer Remotely Piloted Vehicle (RPV). Pioneer had been selected to fulfil the short range RPV role, conducting gunnery spotting from Iowa-class battleships; its accelerated introduction was accomplished under project 'Quick Go'. During October–November 1986, VC-6 RPV Det 1 first tested Pioneer's Rocket Assisted Take Off (RATO) system, the auto-land system and the shipboard Net Retrieval System. In December VC-6 RPV Det 1 went aboard USS Iowa (BB-61) for a five-day proof of concept deployment, becoming the first unit to launch and recover RPVs from a surface combatant. Pioneer was successfully recovered aboard Iowa at night for the first time on 18 October 1987. The first extended deployment of the system began on 3 November 1987, immediately demonstrating the system's value. Adjustments to naval gunfire made as a result of Pioneer-generated information greatly reduced the number of rounds required to destroy simulated targets, while Battleship Battlegroup surface surveillance capabilities were greatly enhanced. In December 1987 the initial development of coordinated RPV/SH-2F tactics began. VC-6 RPV Det 1 eventually operated two systems, each system consisting of a ground control station, a portable control station, five Pioneer air vehicles, plus miscellaneous support equipment.

Personnel from VC-6, RPV Detachment 1, prepare a Pioneer RPV for flight on the deck of the battleship USS *Iowa* (BB 61) on 16 September 1988. Pioneer, which carried a stabilized television camera and a laser designator, was being tested aboard the *Iowa* as a gunnery spotting system, providing over-the-horizon targeting and reconnaissance capabilities. Pioneer had an endurance of eight hours and could be operated out to a range of 110 miles from the Battleship Battlegroup (BBBG), alternatively known as a Surface Action Group (SAG). (NARA)

Naval Air Reserve squadron VP-68 (LW) was also aboard Patuxent River, operating nine P-3As, rising to eleven by 1983. VP-68 began transitioning to P-3B TACNAVMODs during 1984. However, on 1 April 1985, before the transition was complete, VP-68 was relocated from Patuxent River to NAF Washington (q.v.), in order to make room at Patuxent River ready for the Bell Boeing V-22 Osprey tilt-rotor programme.

Patuxent River's station flight (7A) operated one HH-46A and one CH-46A, adding a UC-12B during 1980. During 1981 the HH-46As rose to four, and during 1982 the CH-46A was withdrawn. By April 1983 it operated two HH-46As, one UC-12B, two SH-3Ds and one SH-3G; by October 1983 only the UC-12B and two SH-3Ds remained, rising to four SH-3Ds by 1984. During 1987 the UC-12B and three SH-3Gs were on strength, and by 1989 the UC-12B, two SH-3Gs, three SH-3Ds and two SH-3Hs were operated.

Patuxent River supported OLF Webster, 10 miles south of Patuxent River. OLF Webster accommodated the Naval Electronic Systems Engineering Activity (NAVELEXSYSENGACT), which also operated a single leased Piper Navajo until 1980.

NAS Point Mugu, California

Point Mugu was home to the Pacific Missile Test Center (PACMISTESTCEN or PMTC), under NAVAIR. PMTC was responsible for the development of all USN missile systems, including testing compatibility of new aircraft types with existing missiles. Live weapons were tested over the large nearby Sea Test Range. PMTC operated a fleet of aircraft to conduct and support these tests, including drones. Drones were flown manned from Point Mugu to the small airfield on San Nicolas Island (OLF San Nicolas Island, which Point Mugu supported); once there, the drone was launched on its unmanned mission, and recovered there if it survived.

In April 1980 PMTC operated one A-4M, two TA-4Js, three NRA-3Bs, one NA-3B, one RA-3B, four A-6Es, one NA-6A, three F-4Js, one NF-4J, one F-4N, ten F-14As, four ES-2Ds, one S-2E, one S-2G, two EP-3As, one RP-3A and one T-39D. Also operated were one QT-33A, one QF-86F and three QF-4B drones, along with two DT-2C drone directors.

PMTC's unique bulbous-nosed NRA-3B BuNo 144825, seen with its wings folded at NAS Point Mugu on 5 April 1982. Twin chaff dispensers are mounted under the wing. (NARA)

Above: PMTC F-4J BuNo 153074 in the overall FS 16440 Light Gull Gray scheme on approach to NAS Point Mugu on 31 March 1982. (NARA)

Left: PMTC TA-7C BuNo 156787 carrying a Radar Simulating Set RSS-JEEP pod on the number one pylon, in front of Building 351 at Point Mugu on 27 June 1982. (NARA)

A PMTC A-6E about to be loaded with an AQM-37A air-launched supersonic target drone at Point Mugu on 17 September 1981. (NARA)

PMTC F-14A BuNo 158625 prior to the test launch of an early development Advanced Medium Range Air-to-Air Missile (AMRAAM) on 8 June 1982. Intended to replace the AIM-7 Sparrow medium range air-to-air missile, AMRAAM's development was very protracted; it eventually entered service, as the AIM-120, in 1991. Although it eventually very successfully equipped a wide range of aircraft types, the AIM-120 AMRAAM was ultimately not integrated with the F-14, which retained the AIM-7 until retirement, alongside the short-range AIM-9 and long-range AIM-54. (NARA)

PMTC QF-4B BuNo 149434 in flight on 8 July 1983. QF-4Bs were finished in overall FS 12197 International Orange and were known as 'redbirds'. Although QF-4Bs were target drone conversions, most sorties were flown manned, in conjunction with cheaper sub-scale unmanned drones, due to the relative expense of these full-sized drone conversions. Consequently 149434 is here being flown manned, and is about to launch an AQM-37A target drone. QF-4B 149434 was finally expended as an unmanned target on 19 January 1984; at the time of its destruction 149434 had been the last of the original twelve QF-4Bs converted, and the oldest F-4 in the active Navy inventory. These first twelve QF-4Bs had completed fifty-eight unmanned sorties since the first had been delivered in 1972, as well as a far larger number of manned sorties. (NARA)

By April 1985 PMTC operated five NRA-3Bs, one NA-3B, six A-6Es, one A-7C, one TA-7C, three F-4Js, one F-4N, one F-4S, six F-14As, five EP-3As and three RP-3As, along with ten QF-86Fs, one QF-4J and one QF-4N drones. PMTC received its first F/A-18 later that year.

By October 1987 PMTC operated three NRA-3Bs, one NA-3B, two A-6Es, one A-7C, three TA-7Cs, two F-4Js, two F-4Ss, five F-14As, four F/A-18As, one F/A-18B, four EP-3As and three RP-3As, alongside three QF-4N and seven QF-86F drones.

Also aboard Point Mugu was VX-4 (XF), which conducted test and evaluation of USN operational air-to-air fighter types. VX-4 was under Fighter/Airborne Early Warning Wing Pacific (FITAEWWINGPAC), until 1986 when it fell directly under AirPac. In April 1980 VX-4 operated five F-4Js, one F-4S, ten F-14As, two TA-4Js and one C-1A. Three pre-production F/A-18s joined VX-4 from 1981. By October 1985 VX-4 operated three F-4Ss, eight F-14As and four F/A-18As; by October 1988 they operated three F-4Ss, twelve F-14As, two F/A-18As and two F/A-18Cs.

Deployable units aboard Point Mugu were Antarctic Development Squadron VXE-6 (XD) and Tactical Electronic Warfare Squadron VAQ-34 (GD).

VXE-6 supported Operation Deep Freeze, which was the operational element of the United States Antarctic Program, the latter being the US government organisation undertaking Antarctic scientific research and managed by the National Science Foundation (NSF). To conduct these duties, VXE-6 utilised forward operating bases at Christchurch, New Zealand, and McMurdo Station, Antarctica. VXE-6 operated two LC-130Fs, five LC-130Rs and seven UH-1Ns in 1980. The LC-130F and LC-130R

F-4S BuNo 155539 of VX-4 'Evaluators' at NAS Point Mugu in 1982. VX-4 generally maintained one Phantom in this special scheme as the squadron flagship, usually with the MODEX number '1'. The scheme consisted of overall FS 17038 gloss black, with a FS 37038 matt black anti-glare panel in-front of the canopy, complete with Playboy Bunny tail markings. The specially marked aircraft was nicknamed the 'Black Bunny' and used the call-sign 'Vandy 1'. F-4J BuNo 153783 had been the original 'Black Bunny', which F-4S BuNo 155539 replaced from 1981 until it was retired to AMARC on 2 May 1986. F-4S BuNo 158358 took over during 1987–88 and finally F-4S BuNo 158360 during 1989–90. VX-4's F-14A BuNo 161444 was also temporarily painted in a washable matt black version of the Black Bunny scheme for the 1987 Point Mugu air show. (USN)

A VX-4 TA-4J at Point Mugu on 30 September 1982; it carries an ATM-84 (the training version of the AGM-84 Harpoon anti-ship missile) on the centreline. (NARA)

were ski-equipped, four and six of which had originally been delivered to the USN, but two LC-130Fs and an LC-130R had been lost in accidents in Antarctica during 1971 and 1973. One of those LC-130Fs (BuNo 148321) had been lost taking off from a remote site in East Antarctica on 4 December 1971, when two of its JATO (jet-assisted take-off) bottles separated from the left-hand side of the fuselage striking the inboard engine and propeller. The aircraft was seriously damaged and stranded in Antarctica. In 1986 the decision was made to attempt to recover 148321, by now almost entirely buried in snow, and return it to service. Ironically, and tragically, while supporting 148321's recovery, LC-130R BuNo 159131 crashed while delivering spares on 9 December 1987, killing two and injuring nine. Following recovery and repair, LC-130F 148321 finally flew out of its crash site on 10 January 1988, seventeen years after its mishap, although it would not return to service with VXE-6 until 1993. VXE-6's UH-1N fleet fluctuated between four and seven throughout the 1980s.

VAQ-34 was established on 1 March 1983, to provide electronic warfare (EW) aggressors for training exercises. VAQ-34 was assigned to AirPac, but operationally controlled by the Fleet Electronic Warfare Support Group (FEWSG). Prior to VAQ-34's establishment, the East Coast's VAQ-33 homeported aboard NAS Key West, Florida, provided these services to both coasts. Demand for VAQ-33's services resulted in the

VXE-6 'Puckered Penguins' LC-130R BuNo 160741 taxis past a USAF C-141B Starlifter in Antarctica on 16 November 1988. The scheme consisted of FS 16081 Engine Gray topsides, FS 16440 Light Gull Gray undersides and FS 12197 International Orange wing and fuselage panels. (NARA)

A VXE-6 UH-1N departs on
a scientific support mission
after refuelling at Marble Point
Air Facility during Operation
Deep Freeze on 15 June 1988.
VXE-6's UH-1Ns featured
overall FS 12197 International
Orange. (NARA)

VXE-6 LC-130F BuNo 148321 seen stranded in the ice on 1 November 1987, where it had been since crashing
at the remote East Antarctica site in 1971, and still displaying VXE-6's old JD tailcode. In January 1987 the
National Science Foundation, which managed the United States Antarctic Program and used VXE-6's
aircraft to transport researchers and their equipment, excavated 148321 and determined that it would be less
expensive to repair it than to buy a new one. The rebuilt LC-130F was flown from the crash site on 10 January
1988. (NARA)

establishment of VAQ-34 as a dedicated West Coast electronic aggressor squadron.
VAQ-34 operated one KA-3B, three ERA-3Bs (with a fourth added during 1984) and
six EA-7Ls (TA-7Cs modified as EW aggressors). This allocation of aircraft remained
steady during the remainder of the decade, with a single TA-7C added by 1988.
VAQ-34 was the final USN Skywarrior squadron to establish.

Reserve units aboard Point Mugu were VA-305, VP-65 (PG) and Helicopter Light
Attack Squadron HAL-5 (NW).

VAQ-34 'Flashbacks' operated a single
KA-3B, BuNo 138944, seen here taxiing in
at NAS Dallas on 1 February 1988. This was
VAQ-34's first aircraft after it was established
on 1 March 1983, and had been recovered
from the Military Aircraft Storage and
Disposal Center (MASDC, later redesignated
the Aerospace Maintenance and Regeneration
Center, AMARC) at Davis-Monthan AFB
and brought back to operational status for use
by VAQ-34. (NARA)

Above: Two VAQ-34 EA-7Ls on the ramp at Elmendorf AFB, Alaska, on 8 November 1987 while deployed for the
Third Fleet North Pacific Exercise (NORPACEX). The nearest aircraft (BuNo 156757) carries an AN/AST-4(V)
(AST-4) Radar Emission Simulating Set (RESS) pod (outboard of the external fuel tank), while the rear aircraft
(BuNo 156745) carries the large AN/ALQ-170 Airborne Missile Simulator pod. By this time, VAQ-34's squadron
markings had been modified by the addition of a white lightning bolt behind the red star. (NARA)

Below: VA-305 'Lobos' A-7B BuNo 154474 while deployed to NAS Fallon, Nevada, for training on 24 June
1986. It carries live Mk 83 1000-lb bombs underwing and an Airborne Instrumentation Subsystem (AIS) pod
for the Air Combat Maneuvering Instrumentation (ACMI)/Tactical Air Combat Training System (TACTS)
on the fuselage side; when used over an instrumented range, this allowed training aerial engagements to be
tracked for subsequent review and debrief. (NARA)

VA-305 was assigned to CVWR-30 and operated thirteen A-7Bs. On 1 January 1987 VA-305 was redesignated VFA-305 and began to re-equip with F/A-18As.

VP-65 operated nine P-3As, reducing to eight in 1981 before building to ten during 1982. VP-65 re-equipped with eight P-3Bs in 1986, but retained one P-3A.

HAL-5 was the West Coast counterpart to the East Coast's HAL-4 (aboard NAS Norfolk, Virginia), supporting Naval Special Warfare (NSW) and Explosive Ordnance Disposal (EOD) teams. HAL-5 operated seven HH-1Ks, increasing to eight during 1983. On 20 October 1988 HAL-5 was redesignated Helicopter Combat Support Special Squadron HCS-5, re-equipped with HH-60Hs and added Strike Rescue (Combat SAR) to its primary NSW/EOD support mission.

Left: Three HAL-5 'Blue Hawks' HH-1Ks support the first test-launch of an RGM-84 Harpoon anti-ship missile from the Royal Australian Navy frigate HMAS *Canberra* (FFG 02) in the Pacific Missile Test Center's Sea Test Range on 14 July 1981, four months after *Canberra*'s commissioning. (NARA)

Below: A brand new HCS-5 'Firehawks' HH-60H Seahawk is seen in flight over San Diego, California, on 7 July 1989. (NARA)

A Point Mugu station flight HH-46A hovers as a search and rescue team retrieve a missile booster from the Pacific Missile Test Center Range on 15 February 1983. (NARA)

Point Mugu's station flight operated four HH-46As and two UH-46Ds, adding a UC-12B during 1980. By 1986 it operated three HH-46As, one UH-46D and one UC-12B, this fleet remaining for the remainder of the decade.

Pacific Missile Range Facility (PACMISRANFAC, PMRF), Hawaiian Area, Barking Sands, Kauri, Hawaii

Barking Sands was subordinate to PMTC. The only permanent unit aboard was the station flight, which operated one C-1A, three ES-2Ds (used as range clearing aircraft) and seven UH-3As. The UH-3As reduced to five by April 1981. By October 1983 the C-1A was withdrawn and the UH-3As reduced to four. By April 1985 the US-2Ds reduced to two and a range support Beech B200T was added; by October 1985 the UH-3A fleet increased to seven. The last of the ES-2Ds was retired during March 1986. During 1987 the UH-3As reduced to six. During 1988 the UH-3As further reduced to five and the B200T was replaced by two UC-12Fs.

The USMC helicopter squadrons of MAG-24 at MCAS Kaneohe Bay, Hawaii, deployed around twenty helicopters and approximately 300 personnel to Barking Sands for two weeks twice a year until 1983. Subsequently, both USN Helicopter Anti-Submarine (HS) and Air Anti-Submarine (VS) Squadrons deployed to Barking Sands approximately three times annually to conduct exercises.

Naval Air Development Center (NAVAIRDEVCEN, NADC) Warminster, Pennsylvania

NADC was responsible for enhancing and refining existing aircraft, systems and equipment. NADC was under NAVAIR until 1986 when it was assigned directly to

Commander, Space and Naval Warfare Systems Command (COMSPAWARSYSCOM). NADC was perhaps best known for developing ASW systems, including the development of the systems for the P-3C 'Update' sub-variants, including their passive and active sonobuoys, and the LAMPS (Light Airborne Multi-Purpose System) helicopters (SH-2F LAMPS Mk I and SH-60B LAMPS Mk III). However, it was involved in a very wide range of research and development over the years. This included developing the QF-4B aerial target, the TARPS reconnaissance pod and extremely low frequency (ELF) communications systems to allow TACAMO aircraft to communicate with submerged SSBNs. NADC worked with DuPont to develop flame-resistant Nomex material to replace nylon in flight clothing, and tested the crash worthiness of aircrew restraint systems. In 1986 NADC developed a self-priming single paint coating to replace the standard USN aircraft coating system, which had hitherto consisted of a primer under a polyurethane topcoat.

To support this eclectic range of research and development projects, NADC operated a small but diverse aircraft fleet. In April 1980 NADC operated two P-3As, one YP-3C, three P-3Cs, one C-131F, two CH-53As, one RH-53D, one A-7E and one T-2C. By 1982, NADC operated two P-3As, one NP-3A, one YP-3C, three P-3Cs, one CH-53A, one NCH-53A, one NA-7E and one 'UC-27A' (the unofficial designation for a Fairchild F-27A freighter conversion used by NADC as a utility transport and a project testbed). In April 1985 two UP-3As, three P-3Cs, one CH-53A, two NCH-53As, one NA-7E, one T-2C and one VH-3A were assigned; by 1987 NADC operated three UP-3As, four P-3Cs, two NCH-53As, one NA-7E and one T-2C.

NADC P-3C BuNo 161410 on display at the Patuxent River open house air show during 1984. This aircraft acted as the Update III prototype from April 1983, which was developed at NADC. In 1984 BuNo 161410 was transferred to NATC's Antisubmarine Aircraft Test Directorate at Patuxent River. (NARA)

Marine Corps Continental Fleet Support Stations

The USMC was the USN's sister service, an expeditionary maritime land force, focused on amphibious operations, with 198,500 personnel in 1985, including 8,000 women. Like the USN, the USMC was controlled by the Department of the Navy, one of three Department of Defense military departments. The USMC was not subordinated to the USN. However, while fulfilling different functions, their roles were complimentary, and they were therefore very closely integrated.

Aviation saw the closest USN/USMC integration, through the Naval Air Training and Operating Procedures Standardization (NATOPS) programme. NATOPS prescribed harmonised aircraft operation instructions and procedures to all USN and USMC aviation personnel, improving combat readiness and flight safety.

The USMC was, and remains, noted for its *esprit de corps* and aggressive fighting qualities. General Alfred M. Gray Jr., who was the 29th Commandant of the Marine Corps from 1987 until 1991, captured an important element of this when he stated, 'Every Marine is, first and foremost, a rifleman. All other conditions are secondary.' This was very much the mindset; irrespective of their Military Occupational Specialty (MOS) career field, whether that was in aviation, artillery, armour, engineer, logistics or any other field, all were Marine riflemen first.

The USMC's operating forces included the Fleet Marine Forces (FMF), as well as Marine Detachments (MarDets) aboard naval vessels, Marine Embassy Guards and providing presidential guard and naval shore establishment security.

The mission of the FMFs was to serve with the fleet in the seizure and defence of advanced naval bases, and in the conduct of such land operations as may be essential to the prosecution of a naval campaign. In order to achieve that mission, the USMC was responsible for developing the tactics, techniques and equipment for amphibious operations.

USMC aviation units ('Marine Air') provided the Aviation Combat Element (ACE) within Marine Air Ground Task Forces (MAGTFs). Marine Air utilised rotary-wing and fixed-wing aircraft, and fulfilled six functions: offensive air support, anti-air warfare, assault support, aerial reconnaissance, electronic warfare and control of aircraft and missiles. The rationale behind maintaining an independent 'Marine Air' capability was based on the USMC's desire to retain self-sufficiency, as well as maintaining unified command of expeditionary operations. If Marine Air did not exist, and the USMC had to rely upon requesting air support from the other US armed forces, such requests would be weighed against other priorities. By maintaining an organic Marine Air capability, the USMC not only ensured that air support was always available to support the Marine on the ground, but that it was exclusively focused upon, and tailored to, the needs of the Marine Corps. USMC A-6E, EA-6B, F-4 and

F/A-18 squadrons were also periodically assigned to CVWs for carrier sea deployment, in place of similarly equipped USN squadrons.

The two FMFs, FMF Atlantic (FMFLant), headquartered at Norfolk, Virginia, and FMF Pacific (FMFPac), headquartered at Camp H.M. Smith, Hawaii, were operationally controlled respectively by the USN's Commander-in-Chief, US Atlantic Fleet (CINCLANTFLT) and Commander-in-Chief, US Pacific Fleet (CINCPACFLT). The Commandant of the Marine Corps retained administrative control.

The 2d Marine Division was attached to FMF Atlantic on the East Coast, while the 1st and 3d Marine Divisions were attached to FMF Pacific on the West Coast and Okinawa. Marine Air was also subordinated to the FMFs, administratively divided between three Marine Air Wings and one Marine Brigade; these were further subdivided into Marine Air Groups (MAGs), to which the aviation squadrons were assigned.

Under the FMFs were MAGTFs, which included infantry, artillery, armour, engineer, reconnaissance, aviation and logistics components. MAGTFs were (and remain) balanced, air-ground, combined-arms, task-organised forces under a single commander, structured to accomplish a specific mission. Therefore, they varied considerably in scale, the largest being the Marine Amphibious Force (MAF), through the Marine Amphibious Brigade (MAB) to the smallest, the Marine Amphibious Unit (MAU). On 5 February 1988, the word 'Amphibious' was replaced with 'Expeditionary' to reflect the USMC's changing role in national defence and theatre security, resulting in the replacement terms Marine Expeditionary Force (MEF), Marine Expeditionary Brigade (MEB) and Marine Expeditionary Unit (MEU).

A MAF/MEF was the equivalent of a US Army corps. Commanded by a lieutenant general, it usually included a Marine Division (but could control more than one division if required) and a Marine Air Wing (MAW). It deployed with sixty days of supplies, allowing for sustained autonomous operations. The MAB/MEB's ACE would have usually controlled around sixty A-4s or AV-8s, forty-eight F-4s or F/A-18s, thirty-four A-6s, six EA-6Bs, twelve KC-130s, twelve OV-10s, twenty-four AH-1s, sixty CH-46s, forty-four CH-53s and twenty-four UH-1s. Other MAB/MEB elements would contribute around forty-four tanks, sixty-six howitzers, sixteen I-Hawk surface-to-air missile (SAM) launchers and ninety Stinger man-portable air-defence system (MANPADS) teams. A MAF/MEF would only be deployed for large-scale operations.

A MAB/MEB usually represented the forward echelon of a MAF/MEF, usually consisting of a reinforced infantry regiment supported by a Marine Aircraft Group (MAG) and other elements, with a total of 8,000 to 18,000 Marines. However, the composition of MAB/MEBs could vary widely depending on their assigned task; consequently the MAB/MEB's ACE would also vary considerably.

Smallest were the MAUs/MEUs; these consisted of a reinforced infantry battalion and a reinforced helicopter squadron, totalling 2,000 to 4,000 Marines. An MAU/MEU was usually forward deployed at sea, embarked on five amphibious assault ships and a helicopter carrier. FMFLant and FMFPac each had a MAU/MEU permanently at sea. The MAU/MEU's ACE would normally be based around a CH-46-equipped Marine Medium Helicopter Squadron (HMM), which reinforced its own dozen CH-46s with approximately four CH-53s, four AH-1s, two UH-1s and possibly also six AV-8s, seconded to the HMM from other squadrons to form a composite squadron. This reinforced composite squadron would normally operate from one of the USN's 'helicopter carriers'; the Iwo Jima-class Landing Platform Helicopter (LPH), Tarawa-class Landing Helicopter Assault (LHA) or Wasp-class Landing Helicopter

Dock (LHD) ships. The reinforced composite HMM squadron would have the suffix '(REINFORCED)' or '(REIN)' added to the unit designation for the duration. If the lead squadron did not deploy all of its own aircraft, but was reinforced with aircraft from other squadrons, the dual suffixes '(-)(REIN)' were added.

Under FMFLant was II MAF (II MEF from 1988), headquartered at Camp Lejeune, North Carolina; II MAF/MEF controlled 2d Marine Division (Camp Lejeune) and the 2d MAW (Marine Corps Air Station [MCAS] Cherry Point, North Carolina). It also controlled two MAGTF headquarters: 4th MAB (4th MEB from 1988) focused on Norway contingency operations and 6th MAB (6th MEB from 1988), the Landing Force Sixth Fleet (LF6F) covering the Mediterranean and Black Seas.

Under FMFPac was I MAF (I MEF from 1988), headquartered at Camp Pendleton, California, and III MAF (III MEF from 1988), headquartered at Camp Courtney, Okinawa, Japan. 1 MAF/MEF controlled 1st Marine Division (Camp Pendleton) and 3d MAW (MCAS El Toro, California). It also controlled two MAGTF headquarters: 5th MAB/MEB (Camp Pendleton) and 7th MAB/MEB (Twentynine Palms, California, but with prepositioned equipment in the Indian Ocean). III MAF/MEF controlled 3d Marine Division (Camp Courtney, Okinawa), 1st MAW (MCAS Iwakuni, Japan) and 1st Marine Brigade (MCAS Kaneohe Bay, Oahu, Hawaii; this included the locally based MAG-24 aviation units).

The US Marine Corps Reserve controlled the 4th Division/Wing Team, consisting of the 4th Marine Division (Reinforced) (New Orleans, Louisiana) and the 4th MAW (New Orleans).

The 1st MAW (MCAS Iwakuni) controlled Marine Air Control Group 18 (MACG-18) (MCAS Futenma, Okinawa); MACGs provided the tactical headquarters, air traffic control, short range air defence and air defence control to aircraft for their assigned MAW and MAF/MEF. 1st MAW also controlled MAG-12 (Iwakuni), MAG-15 (Iwakuni) and MAG-36 (Futenma). The MAGs of 1st MAW did not have permanently assigned squadrons of their own; instead, squadrons rotationally deployed from 2d and 3d MAWs.

The 2d MAW (MCAS Cherry Point) controlled MACG-28 (Cherry Point), as well as MAG-14 (Cherry Point), MAG-26 (MCAS New River, North Carolina), MAG-29 (New River), MAG-31 (MCAS Beaufort, South Carolina) and MAG-32 (Cherry Point).

The 3d MAW (MCAS El Toro) controlled MACG-38 (El Toro), as well as MAG-11 (El Toro), MAG-13 (El Toro), MAG-16 (MCAS Tustin, California), MAG-39 (Marine Corps Air Facility [MCAF] Camp Pendleton). It also directly controlled MCAS Yuma, Arizona.

As mentioned above, the 1st Marine Brigade (Kaneohe Bay, Hawaii) controlled MAG-24 (Kaneohe Bay).

The USMC Reserve's 4th MAW (New Orleans) controlled MAG-41 (NAS Dallas, Texas), MAG-42 (NAS Alameda, California), MAG-46 (MCAS El Toro) and MAG-49 (NAS Willow Grove, Pennsylvania).

MCAS Beaufort, South Carolina

Aboard Beaufort was MAG-31, controlling VMFA-115 (VE), VMFA-122 (DC), VMFA-251 (DW), VMFA-312 (DR), VMFA-333 (DN) and VMFA-451 (VM). In 1980 VMFA-115, VMFA-122 and VMFA-312 operated F-4Js, while VMFA-251,

VMFA-333 and VMFA-451 operated F-4Ss. VMFAs generally operated twelve aircraft, although between ten and fifteen could be assigned. MAG-31 deployed one of its VMFA squadrons to MCAS Iwakuni/MAG-15 on temporary six-month rotation duty to 1st MAW under the Unit Deployment Program (UDP).

VMFA-115 put to sea with Carrier Air Wing 17 (CVW-17) aboard USS *Forrestal* during its March to September 1981 Mediterranean deployment, adopting CVW-17's AA tailcode for the duration. VMFA-115 transitioned to F-4Ss from August 1982, then became the first East Coast USMC Hornet squadron, transitioning to F/A-18As by July 1985 with VFA-106, the East Coast USN FRS at NAS Cecil Field. In July 1987 VMFA-115 deployed under UDP to MCAS Iwakuni/MAG-15 for six months from July 1987.

VMFA-122 transitioned from F-4Js to F-4Ss during late 1980/early 1981, and to F/A-18As during 1986.

VMFA-251 transitioned from F-4Ss to F/A-18As during April 1986. VMFA-251 subsequently made several six-month UDP deployments to Iwakuni with its F/A-18As.

VMFA-312 transitioned from F-4Js to F-4Ss during July 1981 and to F/A-18As during 1988. VMFA-312 participated in UDP, deploying to MCAS Iwakuni/MAG-15 during July 1979–January 1980 and January–July 1981 with F-4Js and July 1982–January 1983, January–July 1984, July 1985–January 1986 and January–July 1987 with F-4Ss.

A VMFA-122 'Crusaders' F/A-18A seen on 18 July 1987. A CATM-9L is on the wingtip. Hornets were delivered in the TPS finish from the outset. (NARA)

VMFA-122 F/A-18A BuNo 161971, flown by Lt. Col. P. Sullivan, is seen here about to come to grief after catching fire on take-off while deployed on exercise to Twentynine Palms on 7 February 1987. The centreline fuel tank cap was not properly secured and overpressurised, which blew the cap off and sent fuel into both engines, causing double engine failure. Although 161971 was lost, fortunately Sullivan ejected safely moments after this photograph was taken. (NARA)

Above: A VMFA-251 'Thunderbolts' F-4S taxis at MCAS Cherry Point during the station's air show in 1985. The aircraft has been repainted in the TPS finish and carries a CATM-9 underwing. (NARA)

Right: During April 1986 VMFA-251 transitioned to the F/A-18A; one of their Hornets is seen here a year later on 22 April 1987. (NARA)

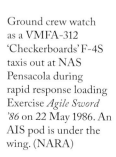

Ground crew watch as a VMFA-312 'Checkerboards' F-4S taxis out at NAS Pensacola during rapid response loading Exercise *Agile Sword '86* on 22 May 1986. An AIS pod is under the wing. (NARA)

VMFA-333 transitioned from F-4Ss to F/A-18As during December 1987. VMFA-333 deployed to MCAS Iwakuni/MAG-15 in July 1981 under UDP.

VMFA-451 made UDP deployments to MCAS Iwakuni/MAG-15 during January–July 1980, July 1981–January 1982, January–July 1983, July 1984–January 1985 and January–July 1986. VMFA-451 transitioned from F-4Ss to F/A-18As during late 1987. VMFA-451 deployed with CVW-13 aboard USS *Coral Sea* (CV-43) during its May to September 1989 Mediterranean deployment, adopting CVW-13's AK tailcode for the duration.

Aviation logistics support for MAG-31 was provided by Headquarters & Maintenance Squadron 31 (H&MS-31). As well as providing aviation logistics support, H&MS-31 (EX) also operated TA-4s for adversary support (although termed as 'aggressors' rather than adopting the more usual Naval Aviation 'adversary' term). Six TA-4Fs were operated in 1980, dropping to four during 1981–82 before increasing to five. By 1985 a TA-4J joined the five TA-4Fs. H&MS-31 was redesignated Marine Aviation Logistics Squadron 31 (MALS-31) in October 1988, withdrawing its TA-4F/Js

Above: A VMFA-451 'Warlords' F/A-18A seen during 1987. (NARA)

Left: An Aviation Ordnanceman (AO) checks a live AIM-9L on the wingtip rail of a VMFA-451 F/A-18A prior to its launch from USS *Coral Sea* (CV-43), while assigned to CVW-13 during *Coral Sea*'s May to September 1989 Mediterranean deployment. VMFA-451 adopted CVW-13's AK air wing tailcode in place of its usual VM squadron tailcode while it was assigned. (NARA)

at this time. MALS-31 completed the transition of its aviation logistics support mission from F-4s to F/A-18s in 1990.

Beaufort's Headquarters & Headquarters Squadron (H&HS) (5B), which, like all H&HSs, reported to the station's commanding officer rather than the MAG, operated two UC-12Bs and three HH-46As throughout the decade.

MCAS Cherry Point, North Carolina

Aboard Cherry Point was 2d MAW and its MAG-14 and MAG-32.

MAG-14's deployable units were Marine Tactical Electronic Warfare Squadron VMAQ-2 (CY), Marine All-Weather Attack Squadrons VMA(AW)-224 (WK), VMA(AW)-332 (EA) and VMA(AW)-533 (ED), and VMGR-252 (BH). MAG-14 also controlled two permanently based training squadrons: Marine All-Weather Attack Training Squadron VMAT(AW)-202 (KC) and Marine Aerial Refueler Transport Training Squadron VMGRT-253 (GR).

VMAQ-2 operated six EA-6As and seven EA-6B in April 1980; by October 1980 the EA-6As had been withdrawn and eighteen EA-6Bs were operated, maintaining strength around this level for the remainder of the decade. VMAQ-2's EA-6Bs were operationally split between three detachments: Dets X, Y and Z. These detachments met rotating overseas commitments, notably the Iwakuni detachment under MAG-12; VMAQ-2's dets also deployed to sea with USN CVWs on six occasions during the 1980s.

VMA(AW)-224, VMA(AW)-332 and VMA(AW)-533 each operated around twelve A-6Es. VMA(AW)-533 joined CVW-17 aboard USS *Saratoga* (CV-60) for an April

A VMAQ-2 'Playboys' EA-6B Prowler seen in flight during 1982. This EA-6B is to ICAP I (Improved Capability) standard, one of a series of progressively upgraded sub-variants. It features the original FS 16440 Light Gull Gray and FS 17875 Insignia White scheme and carries three ALQ-99F Tactical Jamming System (TJS) pods, as well as two external fuel tanks. The large 'football' fairing on the fin-tip contained the System Integration Receiver (SIR) antennas, which detected hostile radars. The system's on-board computer then analysed the information gained and instructed the jammer pods to operate accordingly. The 'beer can' fairing protruding from the rear of the fin-tip 'football' is for the AN/ALQ-126 ECM receiver antenna; this was introduced on ICAP I EA-6Bs, along with another antenna for the same system in a 'sawtooth' at the bottom of the refuelling probe (not visible here). (NARA)

Seen during 1987, this VMAQ-2 EA-6B is to further-improved ICAP II standard. Among other improvements, ICAP II introduced compatibility with AGM-88 HARM missiles, making ICAP II aircraft the first to be armed and therefore gaining a hard-kill capability against radars. This TPS camouflaged EA-6B carries an AGM-88 and an external fuel tank under each wing, with just one TJS pod on the centreline. (NARA)

to October 1984 Mediterranean deployment, replacing VA-85 within CVW-17 for this cruise. VMA(AW)-533 adopted CVW-17's AA tailcode for the duration, and uniquely gained four KA-6Ds to join the ten A-6Es that it deployed with. KA-6Ds were not usually used by Marine squadrons. Later, Secretary of the Navy John Lehman decided to increase the number of A-6E squadrons in USN CVWs from one to two. Two Marine A-6E squadrons were assigned to 'dual A-6 squadron' CVWs from 1985: VMA(AW)-533, as well as El Toro's VMA(AW)-121 (q.v.). VMA(AW)-533 joined CVW-3 aboard USS *John F. Kennedy* (CV-67) for two Mediterranean cruises, August 1986 to March 1987 and August 1988 to February 1989. For these cruises VMA(AW)-533 adopted CVW-3's AC tailcode, and did not gain KA-6Ds, only deploying with A-6Es; its sister squadron during these two cruises, the USN's VA-75, did deploy with their usual mixed A-6E/KA-6D fleet.

VMGR-252 operated thirteen KC-130Fs and four KC-130Rs in October 1980. Strength peaked at eighteen KC-130Fs and four KC-130Rs during 1984; by 1989 nine KC-130Fs and four KC-130Rs were operated.

A VMA(AW)-224 'Bengals' A-6E Intruder seen during Exercise *Kangaroo '89* in Australia during 1989. (NARA)

VMA(AW)-533 'Hawks' was assigned to CVW-3 from 1985, adopting CVW-3's AC tailcode in place of VMA(AW)-533's usual ED squadron tailcode during this time. VMA(AW)-533 joined CVW-3 aboard USS *John F. Kennedy* (CV-67) for two Mediterranean deployments, August 1986 to March 1987 and August 1988 to February 1989. Here a VMA(AW)-533 A-6E TRAM is seen being serviced on the flight line at NAS Fallon on 3 March 1988, during CVW-3's full-CVW integration Strike Det deployment. (NARA)

VMGR-252 'Heavy Haulers' KC-130R BuNo 160625, as seen from a USN RH-53D, which it was about to refuel on 8 January 1982. Depending on if faster fixed-wing aircraft or slower rotary-wing aircraft were being refuelled, different drogue 'baskets' were used for air-to-air refuelling. Here the 'fatter' low speed drogue is seen. This KC-130R features the original scheme of FS 17925 Gloss White topsides and FS 16440 Light Gull Gray undersides. (NARA)

VMGR-252 KC-130F BuNo 148893 visiting MCAS Yuma on 16 October 1989. By now it featured toned-down TPS camouflage, which consisted of FS 35237 Medium Gray topsides, FS 36320 Dark Ghost Gray sides and FS 36495 Light Gray undersides on the KC-130. (NARA)

VMAT(AW)-202 was the Marine A-6 FRS; from the start of the decade until 1984 around fourteen A-6Es and two TC-4Cs were operated; by 1985 the fleet reduced to eight and two respectively. VMAT(AW)-202 was disestablished on 30 September 1986. Thereafter USMC A-6 students passed through the USN's VA-128, the AirPac A-6 FRS aboard NAS Whidbey Island, Washington.

VMGRT-253 was established with six KC-130Fs on 1 October 1986, as the FRS for active and reserve Marine KC-130 aircrew and maintenance personnel.

MAG-32's deployable units were VMA-223 (WP), VMA-231 (CG), VMA-331 (VL) and VMA-542 (WH), with aviation logistics support coming from H&MS-32 (DA) (MALS-32 from 1988). MAG-32 was also assigned permanently based Marine Attack Training Squadron VMAT-203 (KD).

In 1980 VMA-223 and VMA-331 operated A-4Ms, while VMA-231 and VMA-542 operated AV-8As. The number of A-4s and AV-8s assigned to each squadron varied over time, with generally fifteen to twenty assigned, although occasionally as few as nine, or as many as twenty-three. In order to extend the life of the AV-8As pending the arrival of the completely redesigned and much improved AV-8B Harrier II, forty-seven AV-8As were rebuilt to AV-8C standard under a 'conversion in lieu of procurement' (CILOP) programme between 1979 and 1984. Improvements included a radar-warning receiver (RWR), a chaff/flare dispenser, lift-improvement devices (LIDs) and deletion of the nose-mounted F95 oblique camera. The USMC's AV-8A squadrons subsequently operated mixed AV-8A/C fleets until replaced by AV-8Bs.

VMA-223 was the last operational East Coast A-4M squadron, completing transition to the AV-8B on 1 October 1987.

VMA-331 stood down as an operational A-4M squadron on 24 January 1983, ahead of AV-8B training, becoming operational on 30 January 1985 as the USMC's first frontline AV-8B squadron. VMA-331 became the first AV-8B unit to undertake new six-month rotational AV-8B deployments to MCAS Iwakuni, from 6 June 1989.

VMA-231 transitioned from AV-8A/Cs to AV-8Bs in July 1986.

VMA-542 retired its last eleven AV-8As and seven AV-8Cs to AMARC between March and May 1986 and subsequently transitioned to AV-8Bs.

A VMAT(AW)-202 'Double Eagles' TC-4C Academe, used to train student A-6E bombardier/navigators six at a time. (NARA)

A VMA-331 'Bumblebees'
A-4M in the original Light
Gull Gray/Insignia White
scheme with full colour
markings. (NARA)

A VMA-231 'Ace of Spades' AV-8A with temporary washable white snow camouflage added over its usual
scheme and carrying Mk 77 Mod 5 napalm fire bombs, seen deployed to NAS Fallon during 1983. Had the
Cold War turned 'hot', then Marine AV-8s would have found themselves supporting 4th MAB/MEB in
northern Norway where such camouflage would have been essential. (NARA)

With all four VMA squadrons equipped with AV-8Bs by the late 1980s, they built to
a strength of twenty aircraft each.

In addition to providing aviation logistics support, H&MS-32 operated two TA-4Fs,
which were replaced by OA-4Ms during 1980, subsequently maintaining a fleet of
between five and seven. The OA-4M performed forward air control, twenty-seven
having been converted from TA-4Fs; as 'fast FACs', OA-4Ms were more survivable
than OV-10s. H&MS-32 became MALS-32 in 1988.

VMAT-203 was the AV-8 FRS, operating AV-8As and TAV-8As. Between 1980 and
1983 eight or nine AV-8As and six or seven TAV-8As were on strength. The first AV-8B
joined VMAT-203 on 12 January 1984. However, VMAT-203 remained responsible

A VMA-542 'Flying Tigers' AV-8A at Cherry Point. AV-8As were originally delivered in the same British colours as applied to RAF Harriers; BS 241 Dark Green and BS 638 Dark Sea Grey topsides with BS 627 Light Aircraft Grey undersides, along with full-colour markings. From the late 1970s they were progressively repainted in similar US colours of FS 34064 Extra Dark Green and FS 36099 Dark Blue-Gray topsides with FS 36440 Light Gray undersides and adopted toned-down markings, as seen here. (NARA)

A flight deck officer signals to the pilot of VMA-542 AV-8B BuNo 163183 on the deck of USS *John F. Kennedy* during carrier trials on 23 January 1988. As noted by the nose markings, this was the 100th AV-8B. Most AV-8Bs received the wrap-around Land Camouflage Scheme seen here, consisting of FS 34064 Extra Dark Green and FS 36099 Dark Blue-Gray. However, the initial AV-8Bs delivered had those colours on the topsides with FS 36440 Light Gray undersides, which was the same three-colour scheme that AV-8A/Cs had adopted to replace their original British colours. (NARA)

A H&MS-32 TA-4F carrying small practice 'blue bombs' on the underwing bomb rack. Originally Headquarters & Maintenance Squadrons that were assigned TA-4s used them for proficiency flying training by group staff pilots. Later, those Headquarters & Maintenance Squadrons, like H&MS-32, which re-equipped with OA-4Ms, used them in a dedicated Fast-FAC role, still flown by group staff pilots, but now they were also school-trained Forward Air Controllers. (NARA)

A H&MS-32 OA-4M seen flying past Picacho Peak, Arizona, near MCAS Yuma during 1983 in a non-standard experimental camouflage scheme, similar to that used by AV-8A/Cs, rather than the usual grey Tactical Paint Scheme usually applied to OA-4Ms. It carries an LAU-10 four-tube pod for 5-in Zuni rockets outboard under each wing; these were used in its fast-Forward Air Control role to fire smoke rockets to mark targets for other aircraft. Extra air-to-ground radios are in the OA-4M's rear cockpit for communicating with Marines on the ground. (USN)

for training AV-8A/C personnel, as well as AV-8B personnel, until March 1985. By that time five AV-8As, six TAV-8As and ten AV-8Bs were operated; VMAT-203's AV-8As were then withdrawn. The six remaining TAV-8As were replaced by TAV-8Bs from March 1987; the last five TAV-8As were ferried to AMARC during November 1987. By 1989 VMAT-203 operated sixteen AV-8Bs and ten TAV-8Bs.

Also aboard Cherry Point was the Station Operation and Engineering Squadron (SOES), which reported directly to the air station's commanding general. SOES operated two C-9Bs, three CT-39Gs, two U-11As and three HH-46As in 1980. The U-11As were withdrawn during 1982, but the SOES fleet otherwise remained constant during the remainder of the decade. As well as their transport duties, the C-9Bs were also often used as navigation leaders for formations of USMC fighter and attack aircraft when deploying overseas.

Cherry Point housed NARF Cherry Point, renamed NADEP Cherry Point in 1987. Types overhauled were the A-4, AV-8, C-130, F-4, H-1, H-46 and OV-10. This was the only NARF/NADEP located at a USMC, rather than USN, air station.

Left: A VMAT-203 'Hawks' TAV-8A trainer in the original British colours they were delivered in: BS 241 Dark Green and BS 638 Dark Sea Grey topsides with BS 627 Light Aircraft Grey undersides, along with full-colour markings. (NARA)

Below: A C-9B of Cherry Point's Station Operation and Engineering Squadron (SOES). (NARA)

A Cherry Point SOES
HH-46A. (NARA)

MCAS El Toro, California

Aboard El Toro was 3d MAW and its MAG-11 and MAG-13.

MAG-11's deployable squadrons were VMFA-314 (VW), VMFA-323 (WS), VMFA-531 (EC) and Marine Tactical Reconnaissance Squadron VMFP-3 (RF).

VMFA-314, VMFA-323 and VMFA-531 operated F-4Ns in 1980. VMFA-314 became the first USMC F/A-18 squadron, transitioning from August 1982 with VFA-125 at NAS Lemoore, California (which initially served as a joint USN/USMC F/A-18 training unit, until VMFAT-101 later took over those duties for the USMC – q.v.); VMFA-314 became operational on F/A-18As on 7 January 1983. VMFA-323 retired its last F-4N on 14 September 1982, becoming operational on F/A-18As late in 1983. VMFA-531 transitioned to the F/A-18A from January 1983, becoming operational during that summer.

A VMFA-314 'Black Knights' F/A-18A seen with its probe extended ready to refuel on 13 March 1984. VMFA-314 had the distinction of being the first operational Hornet squadron, not just in the Marines, but in US service. (NARA)

A plane director guides a VMFA-314 F/A-18A onto a catapult during flight operations aboard USS *Coral Sea* in the Mediterranean Sea on 29 January 1986, while assigned to CVW-13 during its October 1985 to May 1986 Med cruise. The blotchy appearance which resulted during corrosion work using whatever grey/light blue paint shades were available, typically seen on aircraft in the Tactical Paint Scheme, is evident here. (NARA)

A VMFA-323 'Death Rattlers' F/A-18A intercepts an AV-MF (Soviet Naval Aviation) Il-38 'May' ASW aircraft over the Ionian Sea on 19 January 1986 while assigned to CVW-13 aboard USS Coral Sea. The F/A-18A is armed with live AIM-9Ls and (barely visible here) AIM-7Fs. AV-MF Il-38s periodically deployed to Libya and Syria during the 1980s to cover the Mediterranean; this Il-38 features 'Excellent Aircraft' insignia added to the nose. VMFA-323 joined VMFA-314 for CVW-13's October 1985 to May 1986 Mediterranean deployment aboard USS Coral Sea. (NARA)

VMFA-323 and VMFA-531 deployed to sea with their F-4Ns with CVW-14 aboard USS *Coral Sea* during its November 1979 to June 1980 Western Pacific (WESTPAC)/Indian Ocean (IO) cruise, adopting CVW-14's NK tailcode for the duration; they participated in operations off Iran during the hostage crisis and rescue attempt.

VMFA-314 and VMFA-323 deployed to sea with their F/A-18As with CVW-13 aboard USS *Coral Sea* during its October 1985 to May 1986 Mediterranean cruise, adopting CVW-13's AK tailcode for the duration, participating in the Libya air strikes undertaken during that deployment.

VMFP-3 operated reconnaissance RF-4Bs, maintaining thirteen aircraft with the main unit at El Toro, with three rotationally deployed detachments (Det A, B and C), each of four RF-4Bs. MCAS Iwakuni/MAG-15 was permanently home to rotationally

A VMFA-323 F/A-18A about to catch the arrestor wire while landing aboard USS *Coral Sea* during flight operations off the coast of Libya on 18 March 1986. This Hornet is armed with wingtip AIM-9Ls and under-fuselage AIM-7Fs (again barely visible here), also equipped with external fuel tanks. VMFA-314 and VMFA-323 both participated in the operations against Libya during this deployment. VMFA-323 adopted CVW-13's AK tailcode in place of its usual WS tailcode while assigned. (NARA)

A pair of VMFP-3 'Eyes of the Corps' RF-4Bs in the overall FS 16440 Light Gull Gray scheme. Of the forty-six RF-4Bs built for the USMC, the last three delivered received a more aerodynamically rounded under-nose bulge for the cameras. This not only reduced drag and turbulence, but also increased interior space. The far aircraft here, BuNo 157349, is one such RF-4B; the nearer aircraft, BuNo 157346, displays the more common angular nose underside. (NARA)

deployed VMFP-3 Dets throughout the 1980s. A Det was also permanently rotationally deployed to NAF Atsugi, Japan, with CVW-5 for sea deployment aboard USS *Midway* (CV-41) until 1984.

When MAG-13 moved to MCAS Yuma on 1 October 1987, MAG-11 took over control of three former MAG-13 units which remained homeported at El Toro: VMA(AW)-121, VMA(AW)-242 and VMGR-352. As noted below, VMA(AW)-121 spent the period from 1986 to 1989 assigned to CVW-2 for sea deployment aboard USS *Ranger* (CV-61), then was redesignated VMFA(AW)-121 in 1989 ahead of transitioning from the A-6E to the F/A-18D. VMA(AW)-242 remained A-6E-equipped for the remainder of the decade. VMGR-352 remained equipped with six KC-130Fs and nine KC-130Rs, until 1989 when it operated three and ten respectively.

On 29 September 1987 Marine Fighter Attack Training Squadron VMFAT-101 (SH), formerly the USMC's F-4 FRS at Yuma, moved to El Toro to become the USMC's dedicated F/A-18 FRS. It remained assigned to Yuma's MCCRTG-10 (q.v.), until the latter disestablished on 31 March 1988, and VMFAT-101 joined MAG-11. VMFAT-101 operated thirty F/A-18A/Bs in 1989.

MAG-11's H&MS-11 did not operate aircraft of its own. It was redesignated MALS-11 in 1988 and soon gained OA-4Ms, with four assigned by 1989.

MAG-13's deployable squadrons were A-4M-equipped VMA-211 (CF), VMA-214 (WE) and VMA-311 (WL), A-6E-equipped VMA(AW)-121 (VK) and VMA(AW)-242 (DT), and KC-130F/R-equipped VMGR-352 (QB). The A-4M units each operated between eighteen and twenty-one aircraft. The A-6E units each operated between ten and twelve aircraft until 1984, subsequently operating seven or eight each. VMGR-352

A VMA(AW)-121 'Green Knights' A-6E seen in flight during 1982. This aircraft features the original Light Gull Gray/Insignia White scheme with full colour markings. A red AIS pod is under the wing. (NARA)

A TPS-grey VMA(AW)-121 A-6E TRAM seen while deployed to NAS Fallon for Strike Det on 23 September 1988, while the squadron was assigned to CVW-2. VMA(AW)-121 adopted CVW-2's NE tailcode in place of its usual VK tailcode while assigned. This A-6E carries blue inert training versions of the Mk 83 AIR retarded 1,000-lb dumb bomb and a barely visible AIS pod, as well as a centreline external fuel tank. The Target Recognition Attack Multi-Sensor (TRAM) turret, which the A-6E gained in later life, is evident under the nose. VMA(AW)-121 joined the USN's VA-145 'Swordsmen' in providing CVW-2 with two A-6E squadrons for deployments aboard USS *Ranger* (CV-61) during the second half of the 1980s. (NARA)

operated a mixed KC-130F/KC-130R fleet, which fluctuated during the decade, with four and eight respectively in 1980. By 1982 fourteen and eight were operated, eight and ten by 1983, five and nine by 1984. VMGR-352 settled on operating six and nine during 1985–86.

As well as providing aviation logistics support, MAG-13's H&MS-13 (YU) operated five A-4Ms and one TA-4F in early 1980, transitioning to eleven 'fast-FAC' OA-4Ms later that year, before settling on around eight for the remainder of H&MS-13's time at El Toro, which ended in 1987.

MAG-13 moved to MCAS Yuma on 1 October 1987, VMA-211, VMA-214 and VMA-311 also moving to Yuma and remaining with MAG-13. VMA(AW)-121, VMA(AW)-242 and VMGR-352 remained homeported at El Toro and transferred to MAG-11 control.

In November 1985, VMA(AW)-121 had transferred to the operational control of Commander, CVW-2, attached to USS *Ranger* and adopted CVW-2's NE tailcode. VMA(AW)-121 brought close air support expertise to CVW-2, while developing its skills in areas such as 'war at sea' and providing tanker support. VMA(AW)-121 undertook back-to-back deployments aboard *Ranger* with CVW-2: May to July 1986 (Pacific Ocean for exercise RIMPAC '86), August to October 1986 (North Pacific – NORPAC), March to April 1987 (NORPAC), July to December 1987 (WESTPAC/IO) and February to August 1989 (WESTPAC/IO). By the time VMA(AW)-121 ended its association with CVW-2 in 1989, MAG-13 had moved to Yuma and VMA(AW)-121 therefore fell under MAG-11 at El Toro. As noted above, on 8 December 1989 the squadron was redesignated VMFA(AW)-121, becoming the first USMC F/A-18D Night Attack Hornet squadron, and began transitioning to that new type.

In 1980 the station's H&HS (which reported directly to the air station's commanding general) (5T) operated three UH-1Ns, two T-39Ds and one UC-12B (gaining a second during 1981). A CT-39G replaced the two T-39As by 1982. In 1983 the Station Operations and Maintenance Squadron (SOMS), also reporting directly to the air station's commanding general, took over operating these support aircraft from the H&HS. SOMS added a third UC-12B to its three UH-1Ns and single CT-39G in 1988.

El Toro's Marine Reserve units were under MAG-46, 4th MAW: VMA-134 (MF) operated A-4Fs and TA-4Js, with around fourteen and two assigned. On 1 October 1983 VMA-134 was redesignated VMFA-134 and became operational on F-4Ns during March 1984, transitioned to the F-4S during November 1985, then to the F/A-18A during May 1989, becoming the first Marine Reserve Hornet squadron. VMFA-134 operated around eight aircraft while equipped with F-4s and F/A-18s. HMM-764 (ML) relocated from MCAS (H) Tustin to El Toro during 1983; it operated around fourteen CH-46Es for the remainder of the decade.

MCAS El Toro also furnished limited support to MCAF/MCAS Camp Pendleton (q.v.).

MCAF/MCAS Camp Pendleton, California

The auxiliary landing field at Camp Pendleton, which operated as a sub-unit of MCAS El Toro, became MCAF Camp Pendleton on 1 September 1978; MAG-39 activated on the same date, under 3d MAW, at MCAF Camp Pendleton. MCAS El Toro continued to furnish limited support to MCAF Camp Pendleton. MCAF Camp Pendleton was redesignated MCAS Camp Pendleton on 1 April 1985.

MAG-39's deployable units were HMA-169 (SN), HMA-369 (SM), HML-267 (UV), HML-367 (VT) and VMO-2 (UU). MAG-39's squadrons participated in UDP, making six-month deployments to MCAS Futenma/MAG-36.

During the 1980s the HMA (AH-1) and HML (UH-1) squadrons began to be rearranged with mixed AH-1/UH-1 fleets. Later in the decade both types of squadron were progressively redesignated as Marine Light Attack Helicopter Squadrons (HMLA) to reflect this change.

HMA-169 operated eighteen to twenty-one AH-1Js, replaced with AH-1Ts during 1983, settling on twenty-four aircraft. On 1 October 1986 HMA-169 was redesignated HMLA-169 and received twelve new AH-1Ws (becoming the first Marine AH-1W-equipped squadron) to replace its AH-1Ts, also receiving twelve UH-1Ns.

HMA-369 operated eighteen AH-1Js. From 1983 fifteen UH-1Ns joined HMA-369 and the AH-1J fleet was reduced to ten. On 15 September 1987 HMA-369 was redesignated HMLA-369 and AH-1Ws began replacing the AH-1Js.

HML-267 operated eighteen UH-1Ns; in 1983 ten AH-1Js joined the squadron. It was redesignated HMLA-267 in February 1987, and received AH-1Ws to replace its AH-1Js from March 1987. Illustrating Marine Air's adaptability, during 1988 HMLA-267 divided into three elements, one detachment going on UDP to Futenma/MAG-36, one detachment deployed as part of an MEU, while the third detachment deployed to sea aboard the Austin-class amphibious transport dock USS *Dubuque* (LPD-8); *Dubuque* was the control ship for mine-sweeping operations in the

A HMLA-169 'Vipers' AH-1W SuperCobra takes off from USS *Okinawa* (LPH-3) on 19 December 1987 during Operation *Earnest Will* in the Persian Gulf. *Earnest Will* sought to protect Kuwaiti-owned tankers from Iranian attacks between 24 July 1987 and 26 September 1988; it was the largest naval convoy operation since the Second World War. This AH-1W is armed with a live AIM-9L air-to-air missile as visible here; out of sight on the opposite side it carried a launcher containing four TOW anti-tank missiles. This was a standard load for AH-1s during *Earnest Will*, allowing for both air and surface targets to be engaged. (NARA)

Persian Gulf, protecting US-flagged tankers during the Iran–Iraq War. The HMLA-267 detachment's AH-1Ws and UH-1Ns supported these operations.

HML-367 operated fourteen UH-1Ns, adding eight AH-1Js from 1984; by 1985 it operated eighteen and ten respectively. HML-367 was redesignated HMLA-367 on 1 January 1988, soon receiving AH-1Ws to replace its AH-1Js.

VMO-2 operated eight to ten OV-10As and around eight OV-10Ds throughout the decade.

In addition to the above deployable units, permanently based Marine Helicopter Training Squadron HMT-303 (QT) was established under MAG-39 on 30 April 1982 as the AH-1/UH-1 FRS, operating ten to twelve AH-1Js and eight to ten UH-1Ns throughout most of the decade, later adding AH-1Ws.

No reserve units were at Camp Pendleton until HMA-775 was established under MAG-46 Det E on 7 January 1989, becoming the first West Coast Marine Reserve Cobra squadron, equipped with twelve AH-1Js.

MCAS (H)/MCAS New River, Jacksonville, North Carolina

Marine Corps Air Station (Helicopter) New River was home to MAG-26 and MAG-29, both under 2d MAW. The station was redesignated from MCAS (H) to MCAS during 1985.

In 1980 MAG-26 controlled HMH-362 (YL), HMH-461 (CJ), HMM-162 (YS), HMM-261 (EM), HMM-263 (EG), HMM-264 (EH) and HMM-365 (YM). MAG-26 later gained HMH-464 (EN), which was established on 1 March 1981, and HMM-266 (ES), which was established on 26 April 1983. MAG-29 controlled HMA-269 (HF), HML-167 (TV) and VMO-1 (ER).

MAG-26 and MAG-29 were reorganised during 1982–83 to more closely balance them. During 1982 HMH-464 and HMM-162 were transferred from MAG-26 to MAG-29, while HML-167 transferred from MAG-29 to MAG-26. During 1983 HMM-263 and HMM-365 transferred from MAG-26 to MAG-29. Therefore, from 1983, MAG-26 controlled HMH-362, HMH-461, HMM-261, HMM-264, HMM-266 and HML-167; MAG-29 controlled HMH-464, HMM-162, HMM-263, HMM-365, HMA-269 and VMO-1.

The number of aircraft allocated to HMH and HMM squadrons varied considerably and fluctuated regularly; usually between eleven and nineteen were assigned to each HMH/HMM squadron.

HMH-362 operated CH-53Ds throughout the decade.

HMH-461 operated CH-53Ds, replaced by CH-53Es from September 1988.

HMH-464 was established on 1 March 1981 as the first operational CH-53E squadron. In 1983, a detachment of four HMH-464 CH-53Es deployed as part of HMM-162 (REIN), as 24th MAU's ACE aboard the USS *Iwo Jima* (LPH-2) for the first CH-53E shipboard deployment. *Iwo Jima* operated off the Lebanese coast between May and December 1983 during this deployment, as part of Mediterranean Amphibious Ready Group (MARG) 2-83. MARG 2-83's ships disembarked the main body of 24th MAU to take position in and around Beirut International Airport, relieving the 22nd MAU as the principal US component of the Multinational Force (MNF) in Lebanon. The CH-53Es provided heavy lift support, including providing critical support after the tragic Marine barracks bombing in Beirut on 23 October 1983, which killed 241 US servicemen.

HMM-162 operated CH-46Es; as noted above, as HMM-162 (REIN), they deployed to Lebanon during 1983, supporting 24th MAU's MNF operations, including the barracks bombing aftermath.

HMM-261 operated CH-46Es. As HMM-261 (REIN), 22nd MAU's ACE, they deployed to Lebanon during 1982. In October 1983, just as they were about to be deployed again to Lebanon, HMM-261 (REIN) was instead ordered to deploy to the Caribbean for Operation *Urgent Fury*, the US invasion of Grenada. HMM-261 (REIN) provided assault support during the initial landings and subsequent operations ashore. Two CH-46Es were shot down during these operations. Two attached AH-1Ts were also shot down, with the loss of three of the four pilots. Following operations in Grenada, HMM-261 (REIN) returned to Lebanon.

Two CH-53E Super Stallions from HMH-464 'Condors', while attached to HMM-365 (REIN) and deployed aboard USS *Iwo Jima* (LPH-2). They are participating in Exercise *Ocean Venture '84*, and are seen arriving to airlift 26th MAU Marines from Vieques Island, Puerto Rico, back to USS *Iwo Jima* on 20 April 1984. These helicopters are in the standard overall FS 34095 Medium Field Green version of the contemporary version of the USMC's Land Camouflage Scheme, with toned down markings; this had been in use on USMC helicopters since the late 1970s. (NARA)

CH-46E BuNo 157711 seen abandoned on the coast of Grenada after being shot down by machine gun fire during Operation Urgent Fury on 26 October 1983. BuNo 157711, originally built as a CH-46F, was serving with HMM-261 'Raging Bulls' operating as HMM-261 (REIN). (NARA)

A UH-1N attached to HMM-261 (REIN) touches down in Grenada during Operation *Urgent Fury*. In the background a CH-53D also attached to HMM-261 (REIN) approaches. HMM-261 (REIN) was deployed aboard USS *Guam* (LPH-9), supporting 22d MAU. The yellow square on the tail boom is for the AN/ALE-39 Countermeasure Dispenser System (CMDS) chaff/flare dispenser, one being mounted on each side. These were introduced to Marine helicopters throughout the 1980s. This UH-1N has also gained an AN/ALQ-144 infrared countermeasures (IRCM) jammer 'disco light' behind the main rotor. (NARA)

A CH-46E of HMM-261 (REIN) during flight operations in August 1985, aboard USS *Iwo Jima* in the Mediterranean Sea off Egypt during multinational joint service Exercise *Bright Star '85*. An AH-1T is visible in the background. The weathering to the FS 34095 Medium Field Green finish to BuNo 157660 is notable. The fairing fitted above the rear undercarriage sponson houses the AN/ALE-39 chaff/flare dispenser. (NARA)

A plane director signals to the pilot of an AH-1T attached to HMM-261 (REIN), aboard USS *Iwo Jima* in the Mediterranean during Exercise *Bright Star '85*. Similar to the CH-46 seen in the previous image, this AH-1T has received AN/ALE-39 chaff/flare dispensers above each stub wing. (NARA)

The same plane director seen in the previous image signals to the crew of a CH-53D attached to HMM-261 (REIN), aboard USS *Iwo Jima* during *Bright Star '85*. (NARA)

HMM-263 transitioned from CH-46Fs to upgraded CH-46Es during the summer of 1980. HMM-263 (REIN) served twice in Lebanon: October 1982 to March 1983, and April to August 1984. During 1986 HMM-263 (REIN) served as the ACE of the 26th MAU, which operated in support of Task Force 60 (TF-60) during operations off Libya. They deployed as the ACE for the 24th MAU in May 1987. Contingency operations in the Persian Gulf (supporting Operations *Earnest Will* and *Prime Chance*) required HMM-263 to be split into three sections, operating from the United States, the Mediterranean Sea and the Persian Gulf. In the latter area, aircraft of HMM-263(-)(REIN) participated in the seizure of the Iranian mine-laying ship *Iran Ajr*.

HMM-264 operated CH-46Fs, transitioning to CH-46Es during 1984. They served in Lebanon during 1983, and received the Defense Transportation Safety Award, a Marine Corps Expeditionary Medal, and a Navy Unit Commendation after rescuing numerous Lebanese civilians from the Chouf Mountains, where they had been stranded by heavy snowfall and fighting between Christian Lebanese and Druze forces. During 1987, HMM-264, deployed aboard USS *Nassau* (LHA-4) as HMM-264 (REIN), became the first ACE to deploy with attached AV-8B and MACG elements; these additions to the ACE force list later became standard for deploying LF6F MEUs.

HMM-266 was established on 26 April 1983 with CH-46Es. HMM-266 soon focused on acting as 2d MAW's cold weather assault support experts. Over the following six years HMM-266 participated in fourteen exercises from the Mountain Warfare Training Center (MWTC) in California's Sierra Nevadas, to northern Norway. HMM-266 widened its focus during 1989, adding desert and jungle expertise to its arctic prowess after participating in Exercises Solid Shield '89 and UNITAS '89, Combined Arms Exercises (CAX) at Marine Corps Air Ground Combat Center (MCAGCC) Twentynine Palms, California, and undertaking training at NAS Jacksonville, Florida.

HMM-365 was established on 13 June 1980 with CH-46Es. On 2 December 1986 the squadron reached 80,000 mishap-free flight hours. During 1987 HMM-365 began preparing for its first LF6F deployment, going composite on 1 September 1987. Following workups, it departed as the 26th MAU's ACE aboard USS *Iwo Jima* on 1 March 1988. The deployment saw HMM-365 (REIN) participate in NATO southern region readiness exercise Dragon Hammer '88, amphibious landing exercises (PHIBLEX) in Spain and Italy, and other small exercises in France, Israel and Italy. Returning to New River on 28 August 1988, HMM-365 surpassed 90,000 mishap-free flight hours during the deployment. HMM-365's second LF6F deployment, this time as ACE for the 24th MEU, came during 1989. HMM-365 went composite on 12 April 1989, and departed aboard USS *Iwo Jima* with the 24th MEU Special Operations Capable (SOC) on 12 October 1989. The MEU (SOC) was a new concept, able to undertake limited duration special taskings in support of a combat commander. This included amphibious raids, non-combatant evacuation operations (NEO), security operations, tactical recovery of aircraft and personnel (TRAP), direct action (e.g. conducting raids or direct assaults, standoff attacks by fire from air, ground, or sea platforms, providing terminal guidance for precision-guided munitions) and humanitarian/civic assistance. During the deployment HMM-365 had reached 97,400 mishap-free flight hours before an attached AH-1T was lost at sea. The deployment continued into 1990, with HMM-365 returning to New River on 9 April 1990.

HML-167 operated between twenty and twenty-eight UH-1Ns from 1980 until 1983. HML-167 deployed to Haiti 11–22 August 1980 to provide disaster relief following Hurricane Allen. During 1983 HML-167's UH-1N fleet was reduced to twelve as aircraft were transferred to sister squadron HMA-269. HML-167 achieved ten years/65,000 flight hours of mishap-free flying in October 1983. HML-167 received AH-1Ts from 17 January 1984, with nine UH-1Ns and eight AH-1Ts soon operated. HML-167 became HMLA-167 on 1 April 1986. It was the first unit to be officially designated as a Light Attack Squadron, with a permanent composite AH-1/UH-1 mix. HMLA-167 received its first three AH-1Ws in late 1989.

HMA-269 was equipped with six AH-1Js and fifteen AH-1Ts in 1980. During 1983 it added the utility helicopter support mission with UH-1Ns; it operated twenty-two AH-1J/Ts and twelve UH-1Ns. When HML-167 added AH-1s to its UH-1N fleet during 1984, the HMA-269 AH-1 fleet reduced to six AH-1Js, four AH-1Ts with eleven UH-1Ns. HMA-269 was redesignated HMLA-269 in 1986. By 1989 ten AH-1Ts and nine UH-1Ns were assigned.

VMO-1 operated eleven OV-10As and eight OV-10Ds in 1980; the quantities of both models fluctuated throughout the decade.

A HML-167 'Warriors' UH-1N seen during 1982. This UH-1N still features overall gloss FS 14097 Field Green version of the Land Camouflage Scheme with full colour markings; this had begun to be replaced by overall lustreless FS 34095 Medium Field Green with toned-down marking from the late 1970s. (NARA)

A HMLA-167 UH-1N approaches the Aviation Logistics Support ship SS *Wright* (T-AVB-3) in the Caribbean Sea on 30 March 1988 during Exercise *Ocean Venture '88*. From 18 April 1985 onwards the USMC helicopter fleet began to transition to a new three-colour version of the Land Camouflage Scheme, consisting of FS 35237 Blue Gray, FS 34095 Medium Field Green and FS 37038 Black, as seen on this UH-1N. (NARA)

A VMO-1 'Yazoo' OV-10A seen in flight in 1982. Topsides are in FS 34097 lustreless Field Green, which has here been patchily painted over the originally applied FS 14097 gloss Field Green, while undersides are in FS 36440 lustreless Light Gull Gray. The whole wing, both top and bottom, is painted in white; this made the OV-10 more visible to the friendly aircraft that it was talking onto the targets over the battlefield. (NARA)

A VMO-1 OV-10D seen visiting Cherry Point during 1984; by now OV-10s had adopted overall FS 34095 Medium Field Green with toned-down markings. By the late 1980s they would transition again to the three-colour FS 35237 Blue Gray, FS 34095 Medium Field Green and FS 37038 Black scheme. (NARA)

As well as the above deployable MAG-26 and MAG-29 squadrons, MAG-26 controlled HMT-204 (GX), a permanently based composite training squadron for CH-46 and CH-53 personnel. HMT-204's fleet fluctuated throughout the decade. For example in early 1983 fourteen CH-46Es, nine CH-53As and six CH-53Ds were assigned; by late 1983 HMT-204 had eleven CH-46Es and twelve CH-53Ds. In January 1986 HMT-204 accepted the first of a further enhanced CH-46E sub-variant, the CH-46E Survivability, Reliability and Maintainability (SR&M), to be delivered to the fleet. When HMT-302 (q.v.) aboard MCAS Tustin assumed responsibility for CH-53 training in 1988, HMT-204's CH-53s departed, leaving HMT-204 with ten CH-46Es by 1989.

From 1981 New River's H&HS (5D) gained a UC-12B, with a second added during 1982.

New River also provided limited support to nearby Marine Corps Outlying Landing Field (MCOLF) Camp Davis and MCOLF Oak Grove.

MCAF Quantico, Virginia

The sole unit aboard MCAF Quantico was Marine Helicopter Squadron One (HMX-1), which provided presidential transportation at home and overseas, and which reported administratively to MCAF Quantico.

HMX-1 was functionally split into two elements. The Executive Flight Detachment, known as 'Whiteside', operated gloss dark green helicopters (VH-3Ds and later VH-1Ns and VH-60Ns) with white upper sides (so-called 'white tops') for VIP transportation of the president, vice-president and other VIPs. H-3s and H-60s were unique to HMX-1, and were not to be found elsewhere within USMC service. When transporting the president, the relevant helicopter used the 'Marine One' call sign. The Executive Flight Detachment operated extensively out of Naval Support Facility Anacostia, and was generally tasked by the White House Military Office. The remainder of HMX-1, known as 'Greenside' (operating overall gloss dark green helicopters known as 'green tops') while occasionally providing presidential transportation, generally provided support such as transportation of secret service officials and the press corps following the president, as well as other transportation unrelated to presidential support, and operational test and evaluation. The green tops were CH-46s, CH-53s and UH-1Ns.

A HMX-1 'Nighthawks' VH-3D Sea King lands on the south lawn of the White House on 1 July 1987. (NARA)

Former President Ronald Reagan and his wife, Nancy, walk from a HMX-1 VH-3D at Andrews AFB, Maryland, as they prepare to leave Washington, DC for California aboard a USAF C-137C, following the inauguration of George H. W. Bush as the 41st president of the United States on 20 January 1989. When the sitting president is on board any Marine aircraft, which would usually be a HMX-1 VH-3D, it uses the call sign 'Marine One'; in this case, carrying a former president, it would have used the call sign 'Nighthawk One'. (NARA)

A HMX-1 CH-53D Sea Stallion 'green top', acting as 'Marine One' and carrying President and Mrs. Ronald Reagan aboard USS *John F. Kennedy* in New York Harbor on 4 July 1986, during the Fifth International Naval Review, which commemorated the rededication of the Statue of Liberty. (NARA)

A HMX-1 VH-1N shortly before President Ronald Reagan embarked and it departed as 'Marine One' at the conclusion of the 13th G7 Summit, held in Venice, Italy, between 8 and 10 June 1987. Notable external features differentiating VH-1Ns from UN-1Ns include the extended cabin roof fairing in front of the rotor (adapted from the one found on the Bell 214ST and used to cover the bleed-air, air conditioning system). Two sideways-opening doors replaced the UH-1N's single sliding door on each side of the fuselage. Behind the main rotor is an AN/ALQ-144 IRCM 'disco light'. Internally it was fitted with a VIP interior and upgraded avionics. (NARA)

In early 1980 HMX-1 operated ten VH-3D white tops, and six CH-46F, four CH-53D and five UH-1N green tops. A CH-46E was added later in 1980. By October 1985 HMX-1 operated eleven VH-3D and six VH-1N white tops, and seven CH-46E, six CH-53D, two CH-53E and two UH-1N green tops. Finally, by 1989 HMX-1 operated eleven VH-3D and nine VH-60N white tops, and seven CH-46E, five CH-53D and two CH-53E green tops; the VH-60Ns had been delivered that year, replacing the VH-1Ns.

MCAS (H)/MCAS Tustin, California

MCAS (H) Tustin, redesignated MCAS Tustin in 1985, was home to the HMM and HMH squadrons of MAG-16, under 3d MAW.

HMM-161 (YR) upgraded from CH-46D/Fs to CH-46Es around 1982. HMM-161 made UDP deployments to MCAS Futenma/MAG-36 during September 1980 to February 1981, September 1982 to February 1983 and August 1984 to February 1985. HMM-161 entered into the MAU (later MEU) training and deployment cycle during 1986. It made its first WESTPAC deployment aboard USS *Tarawa* (LHA-1) between 19 June and 19 December 1986. HMM-161 next deployed aboard USS *Okinawa* (LPH–3) on a Persian Gulf deployment between 8 October 1987 and 6 April 1988. HMM-161's final deployment of the decade was to the WESTPAC aboard USS *Belleau Wood* (LHA-3) between 12 January and 18 June 1989. Following the *Exxon Valdez* oil spill in Prince William Sound, Alaska, on 24 March 1989, HMM-161 deployed a CH-46E detachment aboard USS *Duluth* (LPD-6), which conducted oil spill decontamination operations in the area during August 1989.

HMM-163 (YP) upgraded from CH-46D/Fs to CH-46Es around 1981. HMM-163 deployed to MCAS Futenma/MAG-36 under UDP for six-month deployments every eighteen months until 1985; subsequently HMM-163 entered into the MAU/MEU training and deployment cycle for sea deployments.

HMM-164 (YT) became the first West Coast HMM unit to upgrade to CH-46Es, transitioning between November 1980 and March 1981. It deployed to Futenma/MAG-36 under UDP for six months from September 1981. HMM-164 supported the 1984 Summer Olympics in Los Angeles. From early 1985 HMM-164 entered the MAU/MEU training and deployment cycle, before deploying aboard USS *Okinawa* from July 1985.

HMM-166 (YX) was established on 13 September 1985 with CH-46Es, first deploying to sea as the ACE for 15th MAU aboard USS *Tripoli* (LPH-10) between August 1987 and February 1988.

HMM-268 (YQ) had been established on 1 March 1979 with CH-46D/Fs, later upgrading to CH-46Es. HMM-268 made their first UDP deployment to Futenma/

CH-46Es and an AH-1T of HMM-163 (REIN) aboard USS *Peleliu* (LHA-5) during the joint US/Thai Exercise *Cobra Gold '85* during July 1985. The helicopters all feature the then-standard overall FS 34095 Medium Field Green finish. (NARA)

Two HMM-163 'Ridge Runners' CH-46Es bring in more 11th MEU Marines to reinforce those already ashore during the joint US/Thai Exercise *Thalay Thai '89* in September 1989 in Thailand. HMM-163 had adopted 'Evil Eyes' markings on the front of their helicopters during the Vietnam War; by the late 1980s they had reappeared on their CH-46Es. These CH-46Es feature the late 1980s three-colour camouflage; the 'Evil Eyes' are barely visible in this view. HMM-163 was operating as the composite HMM-163 (REIN) at this time, while deployed aboard USS *Tarawa* (LHA-1). (NARA)

A CH-53E, assigned to the composite HMM-163 (REIN), being readied for flight aboard the amphibious assault ship USS *Tarawa* in the Gulf of Thailand during Exercise *Thalay Thai '89*. The CH-53Es, AH-1Ws and UH-1Ns temporarily assigned to HMM-163 (REIN) while it operated as the reinforced Aviation Combat Element of the 11th MEU aboard *Tarawa*, not only adopted HMM-163 titles and 'YP' tailcodes, but also added HMM-163's 'Evil Eyes', as seen on this CH-53E, which also displays the three-colour camouflage scheme. (NARA)

A HMM-163 (REIN) CH-46E departs USS *Tarawa* during Exercise *Thalay Thai '89*. It displays the late 1980s three-colour FS 35237 Blue Gray, FS 34095 Medium Field Green and FS 37038 Black scheme; usually, as here, the amount of black was minimised. (NARA)

MAG-36 from 24 February until 31 August 1980, during which they conducted operations on the Japanese mainland and in South Korea. After their second UDP deployment, HMM-268 was officially designated as 3d MAW's 'Night Assault Squadron' in 1983 and subsequently conducted extensive Night Vision Goggle training. From 1986 HMM-268 entered the MAU/MEU training and deployment cycle, initially deploying as 11th MAU's ACE aboard the USS *New Orleans* (LPH-11). HMM-268 flew over 232 hours supporting the *Exxon Valdez* Alaskan oil spill clean-up operations.

HMH-361 (YN) had added CH-53Ds to its existing CH-53As during 1977, operating a mixed CH-53A/D fleet until 1989 when it settled on an all-CH-53D fleet. HMH-361 made several UDP deployments to Futenma/MAG-36 during the 1980s.

A HMH-361 CH-53A deploys Marines during Combined Arms Exercise (CAX) 1-2-82 at the Marine Corps Air Ground Combat Center (MCAGCC) at Twentynine Palms, California, during November 1981. (NARA)

As well as the USMC helicopters of the Aviation Combat Element's reinforced composite squadron deployed aboard USN Iwo Jima-class, Tarawa-class and Wasp-class amphibious assault ships, a USN HH-1N was also usually permanently assigned to each ship to provide general and 'plane guard' SAR support. This HH-1N was assigned to USS *Wasp* (LHD-1), and used the call sign 'Stinger 1'; it is seen departing *Wasp* in the Atlantic Ocean during December 1989. This HH-1N features the usual scheme for such helicopters of overall FS 16081 Engine Gray with full-colour markings. (NARA)

HMH-363 (YZ) operated a mixed CH-53A/D fleet until 1987, subsequently operating only CH-53Ds; HMH-363 made several UDP deployments to Futenma/MAG-36 during the decade.

HMH-462 (YF) added CH-53Ds to its existing CH-53As from 1983, operating both types together during the remainder of the decade. Like the other HMH squadrons, HMH-462 made several UDP deployments to Futenma/MAG-36 during the decade; during one such deployment in 1989 a HMH-462 detachment participated in contingency operations in the Philippines as part of President Bush's response to Philippine President Corazon Aquino's request for air support during the rebel coup attempt.

HMH-465 (YJ) was established on 1 December 1981 as the first MAG-16/West Coast CH-53E squadron, and the second USMC CH-53E squadron after the East Coast's HMH-464.

HMH-466 (YK) was established on 30 November 1984, as MAG-16's second CH-53E squadron, receiving its first two CH-53Es by December 1984. It had eleven CH-53Es by 30 June 1985, and achieved full strength with sixteen on 5 August 1985.

As well as the above deployable squadrons, permanently based training squadron HMT-301 (SU) was also assigned to MAG-16 at Tustin, operating a mixed CH-46F/CH-53A fleet, with around ten of each early in the decade. CH-53Es were added from 1982, with HMT-301 commencing CH-53E Replacement Aircrew training from December 1983; HMT-301 subsequently established its Fleet Readiness Aviation Maintenance Personnel (FRAMP) department to train CH-53E enlisted mechanics and technicians. By late 1984 ten CH-53Es were operated alongside eight CH-53As and ten

CH-46s. By October 1987 ten CH-46Es, twelve CH-53As and thirteen CH-53Es were assigned. MAG-16 established HMT-302 (UT) at Tustin on 20 November 1987, taking over CH-53 training from HMT-301. HMT-301 therefore subsequently operated only nine or ten CH-46Es, while HMT-302 operated CH-53As and CH-53Es (twelve and eleven respectively as of October 1988, fourteen and ten as of October 1989).

Tustin's only Marine Reserve squadron was HMM-764 (ML), assigned to MAG-46/4th MAW. It operated nine CH-46s, increasing to thirteen by 1983; HMM-764 relocated to El Toro that year (q.v.).

MCAS Yuma, Arizona

MCAS Yuma operated as a joint military/civilian airfield, with the USMC being responsible for all operations and maintenance; McDonnell Douglas also operated a test and training facility from the civilian side of the airfield through an agreement with Yuma County.

Until 1987 Marine Combat Crew Readiness Training Group Ten (MCCRTG-10), under 3d MAW, controlled the units aboard Yuma.

MCCRTG-10's sole deployable operational squadron was VMA-513 (WF), equipped with thirteen to sixteen AV-8As, transitioning to interim AV-8Cs during 1983, and AV-8Bs during early 1987. VMA-513 was originally the only operational West Coast AV-8 unit.

MCCRTG-10's permanently based training units were VMFAT-101 (SH) and VMAT-102 (SC).

VMFAT-101 was the USMC F-4 FRS, equipped with twenty F-4Js and seventeen F-4Ns in October 1980. By October 1981 VMFAT-101 operated thirty-four F-4Js (and no F-4Ns); it began receiving F-4Ss from 1983, being fully F-4S-equipped by 1984, peaking at thirty-three F-4Ss in 1985, and dropping to twenty-four by 1986. When the USN's F-4 FRS, VF-171 aboard NAS Oceana disestablished in 1984, VMFAT-101 took over the responsibility for training the final USN F-4 crews. As mentioned above, VMFAT-101 moved to El Toro on 29 September 1987 (having relinquished its F-4s) to become the USMC's dedicated F/A-18 FRS.

Two VMA-513 'Flying Nightmares' AV-8Cs about to launch from the rolling flight deck of USS *Guadalcanal* (LPH-7) during Exercise *Ahuas Tara II*, taking place in the Caribbean Sea off Honduras in November 1983. This was the first time the *Guadalcanal* embarked Harriers for an extended exercise. (NARA)

A VMA-513 AV-8B is directed on the flight deck of USS *Belleau Wood* (LHA-3) in the Pacific off the coast of San Diego during 1989. (NARA)

VMAT-102 was the USMC A-4 FRS, equipped with twenty-one A-4Ms and six TA-4Fs in April 1980. By April 1984 sixteen A-4Ms and six TA-4Fs were assigned; TA-4Js were added that year, with twenty A-4Ms, seven TA-4Fs and four TA-4Js assigned by October 1984. Numbers of assigned aircraft remained around these levels until VMAT-102 disestablished on 1 October 1987.

While not an aircraft-equipped unit, Marine Aviation Weapons and Tactics Squadron One (MAWTS-1) is worthy of mention. MAWTS-1 was established at MCAS Yuma on 1 June 1978, to conduct aviation unit training, most notably the Weapons and Tactics Instructor (WTI) course. Held twice a year, the seven-week WTI course not only brought together officers from all aviation communities, but also ground combat, combat support, and combat service support officers, ensuring that air-ground interface was appropriately catered for. The course's comprehensive classroom instruction included threat analysis, aviation roles and missions, weapons system employment and integrated operational planning. These lessons were then put to the test in the air, with students' weapons systems employment being evaluated; briefing and debriefing techniques were also reviewed, as were students' airborne instructional skills. At the culmination of the WTI course, a fully integrated combined arms Final Exercise (FINEX) was conducted, combining infantry, armour and aviation units, encompassing all Marine Air functions in support of a notional MAGTF. At the course's conclusion, the newly graduated WTIs returned to their squadrons to share their knowledge and skills. An Aviation Development, Tactics and Evaluation (ADT&E) Department was established within MAWTS-1 in June 1983 to coordinate development and evaluation of tactics and hardware in all areas of Marine Air. In 1988 MAWTS-1 established a Ground Combat Department to encourage increased participation during the WTI course by infantry, artillery and armour officers.

Marine Fighter Training Squadron VMFT-401 was established on 18 March 1986, under direct 4th MAW control, as the USMC's adversary squadron; from June 1987 they received thirteen F-21As leased from Israel. VMFT-401 was assigned the WB tailcode, although this was not used on its aircraft. The F-21As were returned to Israel in September 1989, and VMFT-401 re-equipped with F-5Es. VMFT-401 provided adversary support during MAWTS-1's WTI courses; their work-up to, and participation in, these semi-annual WTI courses taking up the bulk of VMFT-401's annual workload. VMFT-401 also provided adversary support for student F/A-18 pilots training with VMFAT-101, as well as wider adversary support for Marine Air.

Above: A VMFT-401 'Snipers' pilot walks out to his F-21A Kfir ahead of a sortie while deployed to Hill AFB, Utah, during Exercise *Gallant Eagle '88* in August 1988. VMFT-401 included both active duty and reserve pilots. (NARA)

Left: Twenty-five Kfir C1s were leased from Israel during the late 1980s, redesignated as F-21As; twelve were used by the USN's VF-43 and thirteen by VMFT-401. VF-43 adopted the 'Aegean' scheme of FS 35237 Medium Grey, FS 36251 Aggressor Grey and FS 36307 Light Sea Gray wraparound camouflage on all of its F-21As, meanwhile VMFT-401 used several schemes, as seen here. Some wore the 'Aegean' scheme, although as they were repainted they received a simplified 'Aegean' version with FS 35237 Medium Grey and FS 36307 Light Sea Gray topsides, with FS 36307 undersides, as seen on the nearest F-21A. Two desert camouflage schemes were used by other VMFT-401 F-21As. The standard Israeli scheme of FS 33531 Sand, FS 34424 Light Gray Green and FS 30219 Dark Tan topsides with FS 36375 Light Ghost Gray undersides is just visible on the fourth F-21A. A darker scheme of FS 33531 Sand, FS 34102 Green and FS 30219 Dark Tan topside with FS 36231 Gray undersides is seen on the second aircraft. (NARA)

A VMFT-401 F-21A taxis out at Hill AFB during *Gallant Eagle '88*. This aircraft is in the darker desert camouflage scheme. As part of the lease contract with Israel Aircraft Industries (IAI), the latter oversaw F-21A maintenance through Israeli Aircraft Services, which employed eighteen Israelis and eighty US civilians. The contract maintenance achieved an exceptional 99 per cent mission-readiness rate, allowing VMFT-401 to average almost 400 sorties per month. However, the contract maintenance also tied most VMFT-401 operations to Yuma; deployments such as this one to Hill AFB were rare. (NARA)

An Israeli Aircraft Services ground crewman stands by as a VMFT-401 F-21A's General Electric J79-IAI-J1E turbojet is air started at Hill AFB during *Gallant Eagle '88*. The Kfir was notorious for leaking fuel on the ground; the drum on wheels seen here was a standard piece of ground support equipment. Wheeled aside here, it was generally placed under the lowest point of the internal belly tank to catch leaking fuel. (NARA)

When VMFAT-101 transferred to El Toro, and VMAT-102 disestablished, there was considerable reorganisation at Yuma. MAG-13 (remaining under 3d MAW) moved from El Toro to MCAS Yuma on 1 October 1987 (q.v.), bringing A-4M-equipped VMA-211, VMA-214 and VMA-311 with it to Yuma; Yuma's VMA-513, which had re-equipped with AV-8Bs earlier that year, and which was hitherto under MCCRTG-10, was reassigned to MAG-13 upon the latter's arrival at Yuma. MCCRTG-10 itself was disestablished on 31 March 1988. VMA-311 began to replace its A-4Ms with AV-8Bs from 1988; VMA-214 began transitioning to Night Attack AV-8Bs during 1989, the first USMC unit to equip with this sub-variant. VMA-211 completed its last overseas deployment with the A-4M Skyhawk in 1989, then began transferring its A-4Ms to the 4th MAW ahead of transitioning to Night Attack AV-8Bs in 1990.

Yuma's H&HS (5Y) operated three UH-1Ns and two UC-12Bs in 1980. Yuma's SOMS took over operating these support aircraft from the H&HS in 1985; the aircraft fleet remained identical throughout the decade.

A wide range of USN and USMC aircraft routinely deployed to Yuma for training.

A VMA-214 'Blacksheep' A-4M seen on display at MCAS Futenma on 20 September 1988 during Futenma's 'Friendship Day'. VMA-214 was at that time deployed from Yuma to Iwakuni with MAG-12, under its rotational Unit Deployment Program (UDP) commitments. (NARA)

Marine Corps Extra-Continental Fleet Support Stations

MCAS(H)/MCAS Futenma, Okinawa, Japan

MAG-36, under 1st MAW, controlled the units aboard MCAS(H) Futenma, redesignated MCAS Futenma in 1986.

The only deployable squadron permanently assigned to MAG-36 aboard Futenma was VMGR-152 (QD). VMGR-152 was assigned fifteen KC-130Fs in early 1980, reducing to eight by the end of that year; the fleet remained at that level until 1988 when it increased to thirteen. An important role for VMGR-152 was to refuel squadrons of USMC tactical aircraft on trans-Pacific (TRANSPAC) flights between MCAS Iwakuni and their home stations in the USA for their UDP deployments. The USAF took over these duties with the arrival in service of its KC-10As, relieving VMGR-152 of this responsibility, allowing the latter to concentrate on tactical refuelling and transport operations within its local theatre.

The remainder of MAG-36's strength came from squadrons rotationally deployed from Camp Pendleton and/or Tustin under UDP; at any one time, one HML/HMA/HMLA (AH-1/UH-1) squadron, one HMM (CH-46) squadron and one HMH (CH-53) squadron were so deployed.

As well as providing aviation logistics support, MAG-36's H&MS-36 (WX) also operated OV-10s, with four OV-10As and three OV-10Ds assigned for most of the decade.

Above: A VMGR-152 'Sumos' KC-130F refuels USN VC-5 'Checkertails' A-4E during Exercise *Thalay Thai* '89. (NARA)

Right: The crew of a H&MS-36 OV-10A prepare for a sortie on 15 December 1983 during Exercise *Jungle Thunder* while deployed to the USAF's Clark Air Base in the Philippines. (NARA)

By 1988 these seven OV-10A/Ds were given up by the redesignated MALS-36, and operated instead as a Futenma detachment of VMO-2, under MAG-36 operational control.

Futenma's station flight (5F) operated two C-117Ds, replaced by two UC-12Bs in 1981; a CT-39G was added during 1982.

MCAS Iwakuni, Japan

The 1st MAW, and its MAG-12 and MAG-15, were aboard MCAS Iwakuni. Neither MAG-12 nor MAG-15 possessed permanently assigned squadrons of their own, instead 2d MAW and 3d MAW squadrons deployed rotationally for six months under UDP.

MAG-12 was usually assigned one VMA (A-4M) squadron from Cherry Point, El Toro or Yuma, one VMA(AW) (A-6E) squadron from Cherry Point or El Toro, and rotational deployments by VMAQ-2's Dets X, Y and Z (with four EA-6Bs) from Cherry Point.

In order to test USN-USMC interoperability, two USN A-7E squadrons deployed back-to-back to Iwakuni for assignment to MAG-12 during 1984–85, between their usual CVW assignments. These were the first USN squadrons to participate in the USMC's Unit Deployment Program, and the first USN squadrons to come under the command of a Marine Corps officer since the Second World War. While assigned to MAG-12, both squadrons changed their primary mission to close air support (CAS). VA-105 deployed its twelve A-7Es to Iwakuni between July and December 1984. This was followed by VA-37 which deployed its dozen A-7Es between December 1984 and June 1985. During VA-37's deployment, it detached to Yechon Air Base, South Korea, to participate in exercise Team Spirit '85. This was the first time a carrier-based USN squadron had deployed in field conditions since the Second World War.

The only aircraft permanently assigned to MAG-12 were those of H&MS-12 (WA). As well as providing aviation logistics support to MAG-12, H&MS-12 (MALS-12 from 1988) operated six TA-4Fs in 1980; these were replaced by eight OA-4Ms during 1981, with seven or eight operated for the remainder of the decade.

A VMA(AW)-332 'Moonlighters' A-6E visiting Futenma for its 'Friendship Day' on 20 September 1988; the 'Moonlighters' were at that time deployed from their home station of Cherry Point for temporary assignment to MAG-12 at Iwakuni under the squadron's rotational UDP commitments. (NARA)

Above: A H&MS-12 OA-4M taxiing at U-Tapao Royal Thai Navy Airfield, Thailand, while deployed there during Exercise *Thalay Thai '89*. (NARA)

Right: Three of four Iwakuni station flight C-117Ds taxi to the runway to prepare for take-off and a formation flypast over Iwakuni by all four of the flight's C-117Ds on 15 June 1981. With the retirement of Futenma station flight's C-117Ds during 1981, Iwakuni became the last Marine air station to operate C-117Ds. (NARA)

MAG-15 was usually assigned two VMFA (F-4, or from 1988 F/A-18) squadrons from Beaufort, El Toro or Kaneohe Bay and rotational deployments by VMFP-3's Dets A, B and C (with four RF-4Bs) from El Toro. MAG-15 was disestablished on 31 December 1988; MAG-12 then took over MAG-15s former responsibilities controlling deployed VMFA squadrons and VMFP-3 Dets.

Iwakuni's station flight (5G) operated three HH-46As throughout the decade, plus four C-117Ds, which were replaced by two UC-12Bs by 1983.

MCAS Kaneohe Bay, Oahu, Hawaii

Kaneohe Bay was home to 1st Marine Brigade and its MAG-24, which controlled three VMFAs, three (later four) HMMs and one HMM.

VMFA-212 (WD) operated F-4Js in 1980, transitioning to F-4Ss in February 1981 before transitioning to F/A-18Cs with VMFAT-101 during 1988–89, completing the process by April 1989, to become the first operational Marine F/A-18C squadron.

VMFA-232 (WT) operated F-4Ss in 1980. Their last F-4Ss left Kaneohe Bay on 11 October 1988; they took part in exercises in the USA for six weeks with their Phantoms, before undergoing Hornet training with VFMAT-101 from November 1988, becoming MAG-24's second F/A-18C unit in mid-1989.

VMFA-235 (DB) operated F-4Js in 1980. From November 1981 to January 1982 they transitioned to F-4Ss. The last F-4Ss of VMFA-235 (and MAG-24) left Kaneohe Bay on 2 February 1989; they then took part in a Red Flag exercise at Nellis AFB, Nevada, before standing down as the final operational naval aviation F-4 fighter squadron and retiring their F-4Ss to AMARC. They then underwent Hornet training with VFMAT-101 during the summer and returned to Kaneohe Bay with F/A-18Cs by September 1989, as MAG-24's third and final F/A-18C squadron. Each VMFA squadron usually had twelve aircraft assigned. MAG-24's VMFA squadrons periodically participated in UDP six-month deployments to Iwakuni.

HMM-165 (YW) operated CH-46Ds, upgrading to CH-46Es around 1982. In 1981, HMM-165 (REIN) deployed to the WESTPAC and Arabian Sea as 31st MAU's ACE aboard USS *Belleau Wood*. From April 1983 HMM-165 (REIN) once again deployed as 31st MAU's ACE, now aboard USS *Tarawa*, to the WESTPAC/IO, visiting Okinawa, the Philippines, Thailand, Malaysia, Kenya, and Somalia. USS *Tarawa* was diverted to Beirut, Lebanon, during September and October 1983 where HMM-165 (REIN) conducted contingency operations; they returned to Kaneohe Bay before the end of the year. HMM-165 conducted operations in the Philippines during the coup attempt there in December 1989, including reinforcement of the US Embassy.

A VMFA-235 'Death Angels' F-4S on the flight line at NAS Cubi Point in the Philippines while deployed there during May 1982. VMFA-235 had completed transition from F-4Js to F-4Ss earlier in 1982. This F-4S is in the overall FS 16440 Light Gull Gray scheme; a NAN-2 nitrogen servicing unit is in the foreground. (NARA)

HMM-262 (ET) operated CH-46Fs. HMM-262 (REIN) deployed as 17th MAU's ACE aboard USS *New Orleans* in May 1980 to conduct contingency operations in the northern Persian Gulf in response to the Iran hostage crisis. From July 1981 HMM-262 (REIN) deployed to the WESTPAC aboard USS *Okinawa*; during this deployment they diverted to again conduct operations in the northern Persian Gulf, this time to support Afghanistan contingency operations. Before concluding this deployment they conducted exercises off Kenya and Australia. During March–April 1982 HMM-262 transitioned from CH-46Fs to CH-46Es, deploying to the WESTPAC/IO with their new mounts, as HMM-262 (REIN) aboard USS *Belleau Wood* from September 1982 to February 1983. This deployment saw HMM-262 (REIN) participate in an exercise in Oman. They also took part in the first visit by US forces to Somalia since the 1977 Soviet-Somali split, undertaking an amphibious exercise and conducting a port visit to Berbera. Before the conclusion of this deployment HMM-262 (REIN) participated in exercise Valiant Usher 83-2 in Perth, Australia, transporting over 2,200 personnel and half a million pounds of external cargo, conducting 332 flying hours over four days. HMM-262 (REIN) deployed aboard USS *Peleliu* (LHA-5) from September 1983 as 31st MAU's ACE, participating in exercises off Iwo Jima and South Korea. HMM-262 (REIN) deployed again as 31st MAU's ACE, this time aboard USS *Tarawa* from October 1984 to April 1985; this was the final shipboard deployment for a Kaneohe Bay/MAG-24 unit. HMM-262 entered the Unit Deployment Program, making its first deployment to MCAS Futenma/MAG-36 in 1986. In August 1987 HMM-262 transitioned from CH-46Es to the further improved CH-46E (SR&M). In August 1988 they again deployed to Futenma/MAG-36 under UDP.

CH-46D-equipped HMM-265 (EP) completed a WESTPAC deployment, as HMM-265 (REIN) in February 1980. This had seen them deploy aboard USS *Tripoli* for operations off Okinawa, Australia, New Guinea and Hong Kong. HMM-265 (REIN) deployed with USS *Tarawa* from October 1980, visiting the Philippines, Singapore, Diego Garcia, Australia and South Korea, before returning to Kaneohe Bay during April 1981. HMM-265 later transitioned to CH-46Es, and like the other MAG-24 CH-46 units, it ceased shipboard deployments and undertook UDP deployments to Futenma/MAG-36 during the second half of the 1980s.

An additional CH-46 squadron, HMM-364 (PF), was established on 28 September 1984 equipped with CH-46Es.

HMH-463 (YH) operated CH-53Ds throughout the decade, with eleven operated in April 1980. The number assigned fluctuated throughout the decade, with as few as four being on strength in October 1980, but generally seven to twelve were assigned. By 1987 thirteen were assigned, rising to fourteen by 1989. Unusually HMH-463 was also assigned UH-1Ns for at least part of the decade, with six assigned in April 1980.

Camp Pendleton's HML-367 operated a detachment aboard Kaneohe Bay between 1982 and around 1987. The HML-367 Det operated up to six UH-1Ns from Kaneohe Bay, and presumably took over operating UH-1Ns from HMH-463 during this period.

As well as providing aviation logistics support to MAG-24, H&MS-24 (EW) also operated TA-4Fs until around 1988 (when H&MS-24 became MALS-24). From 1980 until 1985 three or four were on strength, rising to five from 1985 until around 1988.

The Station Operations and Maintenance Squadron (SOMS), which reported to the station's commanding officer, operated up to four HH-46As until 1987 when the first of four HH-46Ds began to replace the HH-46As; a UC-12B was also added during 1987.

Bibliography

Cole, Ronald H., *Operation Urgent Fury* (Washington: Joint History Office, Office of the Chairman of the Joint Chiefs of Staff, 1997)

Cooper, Tom; Delalande, Arnaud and Grandolini, Albert, *Libyan Air Wars Parts 1, 2 and 3* (Solihull: Helion & Company Limited, 2014/16)

Crutch, Mike, *CVW: US Navy Carrier Air Wing Aircraft 1975-2015 Volume One Fifth Edition* (A9Aviation, 2020)

Donald, David (ed.), *US Navy & Marine Corps Air Power Directory* (London: Aerospace Publishing Limited, 1992)

Donald, David and Marsh, Daniel J., *Carrier Aviation Air Power Directory* (Norwalk: AIRtime Publishing Inc. 2001)

Evans, Mark L. and Grossnick, Roy A., *United States Naval Aviation 1910–2010 Volumes I and II* (Washington, DC: Naval History and Heritage Command, Department of the Navy, 2015)

Grossnick, Roy A., *United States Naval Aviation 1910–1995* (Washington DC: Naval Historical Center, Department of the Navy, 1997)

Mersky, Peter, Commander USNR-R, *U.S. Naval Air Reserve* (Washington, DC: Deputy Chief of Naval Operations (Air Warfare) and the Commander, Naval Air Systems Command, 1987)

Romano, Angelo, *Electronic Aggressors Part Two (1978-2000)* (Simi Valley: Ginter Books 2019)

Stewart, Chuck, *Aggressor Aircraft* (London: Osprey Publishing Limited, 1990)

Trotti, John, *Marine Air: First To Fight* (Novato: Presidio Press 1985)

Journals and Periodicals

World Air Power Journal, various volumes (Aerospace Publishing Limited)

Unpublished Papers

Reflector, Volume 28, Number 3, March 1984 (Naval Air Development Center, Warminster, PA)

OPNAV Notice C5400: Promulgation of Naval Aeronautical Organization (April 1980 through October 1989 publications)

P-3 Aircraft Location History Report (P-3 Orion Research Group - The Netherlands, 2021)